The Living Birth Chart

Astrological Psychology: A Practical Workbook

Joyce Hopewell

HopeWell
Knutsford, England

First published in the U.K. in 2008 by HopeWell

HopeWell
PO Box 118, Knutsford
Cheshire WA16 8TG, U.K.

Copyright © Joyce Hopewell 2008

All rights reserved. No part of this publication may be reproduced, sorted in a retrieval system, or transmitted in any form or by any means, electronic or otherwise, without the prior permission of the publisher. Reviewers may quote brief passages.

Edited by Barry Hopewell

ISBN 978-0-9547680-9-6

Dedicated to

Bruno and Louise Huber, pioneers of this wonderful new synthesis of astrology and modern growth psychology,

and to

Richard Llewellyn, who was instrumental in bringing their teaching to the English-speaking world.

Acknowledgements

I would like to thank all who have contributed to the development of this book in any way, particularly 'Gareth', 'May', 'Dan' and 'Penny' for their feedback in Chapters 2-4, and 'Sarah', 'Rachel', 'Claire' and 'Clara' for being the co-operative subjects of the interpretations in Chapters 5 and 7.

Thanks also go to my teachers: Richard Llewellyn, Alice Llewellyn, Joan Swallow, Jonathan Powell, Val Burnham, Brian Vickery and, of course, Bruno and Louise Huber.

I would also like to thank all those students of astrological psychology who have attended my workshops and tried out the exercises now found in this book.

Contents

Chapter 1

Introduction   1
Overview of the Huber Method   4
The Development of Astrological Psychology   4
The Five Levels of the Chart   5
The Aspects   6
The Planets   8
The Signs of the Zodiac   8
The Houses   9

Chapter 2

Seeing the Whole Person   11
Chart Image   12
   Examples – Chart Image   12
Aspect Colours and Motivation   20
Chart Shaping and Motivation   23
Chart Direction and Motivation   25
Public or Private? – "I" and "You" Sided Charts   28
Aspect Patterns   32
   The Ambivalence Triangle   33
   The Trampoline   36
   The Recorder   38
   The Dominant Learning Triangle   41

Chapter 3

Integrating the Personality   47
The Threefold Personality – The Ego Planets   47
Position of Sun, Moon and Saturn   49

Sun and the Mind   ☉   51
Moon and the Feelings   ☽   54
Saturn and the Body   ♄   58
Practical Work with Sun, Moon and Saturn in the Chart   63
Aspects to the Ego Planets   64
Ego Planet Positioning   66
   Example – Strongest Ego Planet   68

Chapter 4

Integrating with the Environment — 73
The Family Model — 74
Family Model – Theory — 74
   Examples – Family Model Grouping — 80
The Energy Balance – Planets in Houses — 82
The Dynamic Energy Curve — 86
   Example – Planetary Positions — 90
   Example – Low Point Planet — 91
   Example – Cuspal Planet — 92
Innate Qualities and Environment — 94
Sign and House Strength — 94
The Dynamic Calculations — 94
   Example – Margaret Thatcher — 100
The House Chart and Environmental Influences — 103
   Example – House Chart — 110

Chapter 5

Reconciling Past, Present and Future — 113
Using The Three Charts — 113
Moon Node and Natal Charts — 114
Ego Planets in Moon Node and Natal Charts — 119
   Examples of Ego Planets Changing Position — 122
   Worked Example — 124
Age Progression in the Moon Node Chart — 130
Intersection of the Age Point — 131
   Crossing Point Example – Sarah — 134
   Crossing Point Example – Rachel — 138

Chapter 6

Following the Spiritual Path — 143
The Levels of the Planets — 145
The Transpersonal Planets — 150
Uranus — 152
Neptune — 154
Pluto — 156
The Nodal Axis and the Moon's Nodes — 159
The Nodal Axes and their Tasks — 162
Working with the North Node — 172

Sun Sign, Ascendant Sign — **175**
The Ascendant Sign — 178
Esoteric Seed Thoughts for the Signs — 179

Chapter 7

Working with the Three Charts — **183**
Example 1 – Claire — 184
Example 2 – Clara — 198

Bibliography — **215**

Contacts and Resources — **217**

Chapter 1

Introduction

This book is intended as a follow up to *The Cosmic Egg Timer*, where Richard Llewellyn and I gave an introduction to Astrological Psychology and the Huber Method. Many of the topics covered in *The Cosmic Egg Timer* are revisited in greater depth, with an emphasis on working practically with the material presented, as well as working in a hands-on way with your own chart.

Here I share my own experience and understanding of this new astrological approach to psychology, based on twenty-one years experience as an astrological counsellor, teacher, correspondence tutor and training facilitator for the UK Astrological Psychology Institute. The practical exercises and activities suggested for the reader have been tried and tested in live training seminars and workshops, and have brought deeper understanding to the people who have worked through them, together with a lot of insight, enjoyment and laughter, as they learned more about their birth charts and themselves along the way. I've included the kind of questions that students ask me about various aspects of the Huber Method, and I've aimed to respond in a manner similar to the replies I give when I'm teaching, either in a live session or when I'm tutoring by correspondence.

Astrological psychology was developed in Zürich, Switzerland in the early 1960's by Swiss astrologers/psychologists Bruno and Louise Huber. Using their extensive understanding of astrology, psychology, the spiritual teachings of Alice Bailey and Roberto Assagioli's psychosynthesis, they succeeded in combining the very best of traditional astrology with modern growth psychology. Drawing these threads together, and basing their teaching on their own empirical research, the Huber Method evolved organically and is now used by thousands of practitioners and students of astrological psychology throughout the world. It provides a powerful tool for self-understanding and psychological/spiritual growth which is practical, easy to use and which can yield profound insights for the user.

It's very clear to me that the best way to learn and understand astrology from a deep level is to make it come alive in ways that we can relate to. It's all well and good to understand what Mars means on an intellectual level. We have a concept of what kind of energy Mars has, and how it might be expressed. But can you spot Mars in action and for real in your everyday life? Can you observe it at work in yourself and in the behaviour of others? Do you watch a TV programme, film or live interview and see Mars in action in some of the characters? If you can do that, then that's what I call making your astrology come alive and be tangible and "for real". When it becomes an integral part of your everyday life, then your astrology lives, and you do too, in a more consciously aware and responsible way.

The key feature of using astrological psychology as a tool for personal growth and self-awareness is that it places taking responsibility for ourselves, our own lives and what goes on in them, very firmly into our hands and our hands alone. It offers us choice, and once we're aware that we can exercise this in our everyday lives, things are unlikely to ever be the same again. We will be in the driving seat rather than in the passenger seat, and the responsibility for which direction we take will be entirely ours.

This is a practical workbook, and the best way to gain the most from it is to work through the exercises using your own chart. The content is not intended as a course in the Huber Method of astrological psychology, but if the reader is already a student of the UK Astrological Psychology Institute [API(UK)] they will hopefully find the content a useful supplement to the course material. Readers whose appetite is whetted and who want to know more about API(UK) courses in astrological psychology can find details in the 'Resources' section on page 217. Courses for both personal interest and professional qualification are offered.

Regardless of whether you are a student or not, it is recommended that you have a notebook or loose leaf file to use alongside this workbook. You will certainly benefit from working on your own chart, and if you have a few other charts to work on – maybe those of family and friends – this will help expand and deepen your experience and understanding of using astrological psychology, as well as making the learning journey through this book more interesting, insightful and rewarding.

For those unfamiliar with the Huber Method, we begin with an outline of key features of this approach to chart interpretation. Those who are familiar with it, for example from reading *The Cosmic Egg Timer*, may wish to skip this and go straight to Chapter 2 on page 11.

Overview of the Huber Method

The Development of Astrological Psychology

For the past fifty years, Bruno and Louise Huber have worked as pioneers in bringing together the best of traditional astrology with modern growth psychology. They developed their own unique approach to astrology after years of research in collaboration with Roberto Assagioli, the founder of Psychosynthesis.

Bruno and Louise trained with Assagioli and worked alongside him at his clinic in Florence. Whilst there, they drew upon his psychological research, together with their practical experiences with the clients they saw, and used this to test and extend their understanding of astrology. This enabled them to confirm parts of existing astrology and to discover new insights, methods and techniques.

The Hubers developed their own Method of astrological psychology and on returning to their native Switzerland, they established the Astrological Psychology Institute in Zürich in 1962. Their approach is now learned and used in many countries throughout the world, and its applications are found in the helping and therapeutic professions. In 1983, the Astrological Psychology Institute (UK) was formed; it has since trained many English-speaking students in the Huber Method. A list of graduate astrological counsellors can be found at www.api-uk.org.

The Huber Method of Astrological Psychology can help the individual's psychological and spiritual growth process, and facilitate the counselling process as it offers a "fast track" to uncovering psychological problems as well as pointing the way towards resolving them.

> ** If you are new to the Huber Method, and do not already have a natal chart drawn up in the Huber style, you can obtain charts and/or software from the 'Resources' on page 217.

The Five Levels of the Chart

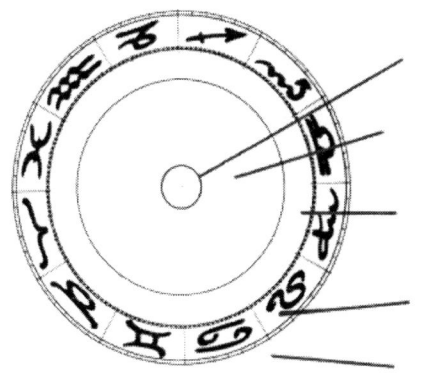

Central Core
(inner being)

Aspects
(unconscious motivation)

Planets
(psychological drives)

Signs
(inherited qualities)

Houses
(the environment)

The Five Levels

- The Central Core of the chart – pure energy, the Higher Self, divine spark

- The Aspects – pick up energy of specific qualities (Cardinal, Fixed, Mutable) from the central core

- The Planets – act like light bulbs, lit up by the aspects; different drives are expressed through them

- The Signs – inherited traits and qualities

- The Houses – areas of life experience; the environment, the outside world

The Aspects

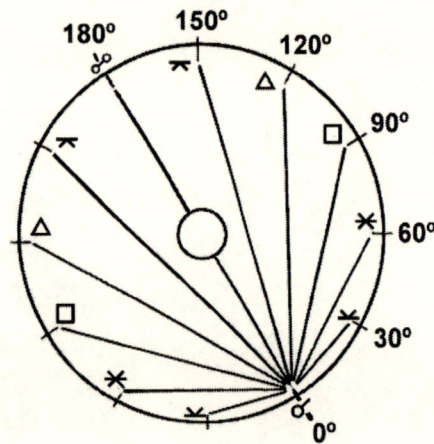

The seven aspects used in the Huber Method are based on the Ptolemaic arrangement, and are multiples of 30 degrees:

0 degrees	Conjunction	☌	orange; close, binding, new potential
30 degrees	Semi-sextile	⚺	green; information gathering, perceptive
60 degrees	Sextile	✶	blue; seeking harmony, compromises
90 degrees	Square	□	red; active, performance oriented
120 degrees	Trine	△	blue; enjoyment, bounty, abundance
150 degrees	Quincunx	⚻	green; questing, searching, committed
180 degrees	Opposition	☍	red; tension, suppressed energy

These aspects form more than 45 **aspect patterns**. Details of some of the more common patterns can be found in *The Cosmic Egg Timer;* details of all patterns are in *Aspect Pattern Astrology*. Basic guidelines for understanding **aspect patterns** are summarised below.

Aspect Pattern Guidelines – Shaping and Colour

Shaping

- Is the pattern Mutable (triangular) or Fixed (quadrangular) or Cardinal (linear)?

- What does this tell you about its motivation?

Colour

- How many colours are involved?

- What are they?

- What does the combination of colours tell you? (e.g. all red; all blue; red/blue; red/green; green/blue; red/green/blue)

- What are the aspect colours inside the pattern? This will indicate what's going on inside, what is less visible.

- What are the aspect colours on the outside boundaries of the pattern? This will indicate what shows on the outside, what is more apparent to the world, and what the person is more likely to show.

The Planets

Sun	☉	Jupiter	♃
Moon	☽	Saturn	♄
Mercury	☿	Uranus	♅
Venus	♀	Neptune	♆
Mars	♂	Pluto	♇
Moon's Node	☊		

* The Moon's Node is not actually a physical object, but is included because of its significance for personal and spiritual growth.

The Signs of the Zodiac

Aries	♈	Libra	♎
Taurus	♉	Scorpio	♏
Gemini	♊	Sagittarius	♐
Cancer	♋	Capricorn	♑
Leo	♌	Aquarius	♒
Virgo	♍	Pisces	♓

The Houses

The First House: Self-image. Exclusively about ourselves, about "me".

The Second House: Security and self-worth; what we possess and what we value in life.

The Third House: Communication. Learning and gathering facts and information.

The Fourth House: Roots, family and home.

The Fifth House: Relationships, pleasure, entertainment, sport, creativity.

The Sixth House: The workplace and the area of life where we can be of service to others.

The Seventh House: One-to-one encounters and partnerships with others.

The Eighth House: Shared possessions; being part of society, paying dues and taxes.

The Ninth House: Expansion of thinking; finding our own truth.

The Tenth House: Individuality. Wanting to be recognised.

The Eleventh House: Ideas; using the mind. Relating to groups of like-minded people.

The Twelfth House: Retreat, withdrawal, contemplation and renewal of energy.

Chapter 2

Seeing the Whole Person

The Whole Chart and the Aspect Level

"Where on earth do I start with a chart?"
Students new, and sometimes not-so-new, to the Huber Method often express concerns about how to begin interpreting a chart. They ask: Where should I start? What should I do? What should I look at first? The most common thing that worries them is if they go blank and don't know what to say. As the approach of the Huber Method is one of uncluttered simplicity, all that is required when starting to work with a chart is to remember to centre yourself, to be fully present, and to focus on the **whole chart**. The chart represents the person – the whole person – so it's important to honour and acknowledge the wholeness of that person's being when beginning any chart work.

Huber-style charts come complete with their own starting point – the circle in the centre of the chart which is always left as a clear space. This empty circle, the central core of the chart, is symbolic of soul, spirit, the Higher Self, God… call it what you will. It represents the place within us where we can connect with an energy source beyond ourselves. Each of us will have our own understanding and appreciation of what that symbolic empty space means for us, and it is here that any chart interpretation should always begin. It doesn't take long to do, but it's very important to acknowledge and include this clear space in the chart which represents the essential divinity of the person.

"OK – that's easy. But what next?"

Chart Image

The next step is to look at the aspect structure of the chart, which represents the unconscious motivation of the person. Here, what you're looking for is an image or picture in the chart, using your eyes and your senses and your intuition. This approach is what we call Jupiterian astrology, where the eyes are used to see, the intuition is brought into play and the astrologer gains a sense of the chart as a whole. Forget the mental chatter of Mercury and forego pitching into instant analysis; allow your eyes to really **see** what is there in the chart, and let your intuition guide you.

Students and newcomers to the Huber Method usually find this a liberating way of approaching charts because they can lay aside whatever astrology they might already know and simply allow themselves to **be** with the chart itself and stay open to what it suggests. Complete newcomers who know little or no astrology find this particularly satisfying as they can very quickly see something meaningful for themselves in their own chart, as well as being able to offer relevant and perceptive observations on the charts of others.

Examples – Chart Image

Here are some examples of the chart images of real people, along with their Jupiterian, intuitive observations on what they see. The first three examples were written by the owners of the charts when they were asked to describe the visual images in their charts.

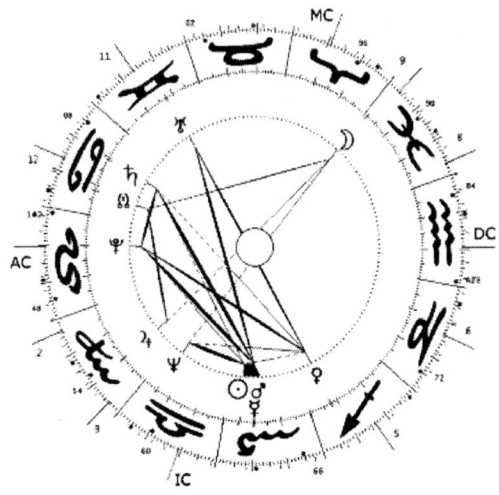

Eric
28.10.1944, 23:45, Lincoln, UK

"I can see three images:

• *A swinging boat with the Moon at the axis. Maybe a loose forecastle and an unnecessary tiller.*

• *A wooden mallet with the Moon at the handle. The mallet has violently struck the 4th house causing great stress at the conjunction of Sun/Mercury/Mars.*

• *Finally, there is a Heath Robinson type of construction trying to prevent the Moon from getting into the 1st, 2nd and 3rd houses. The barrier has failed as there is a clear way through in the gap between Jupiter and Neptune."*

14 *The Living Birth Chart*

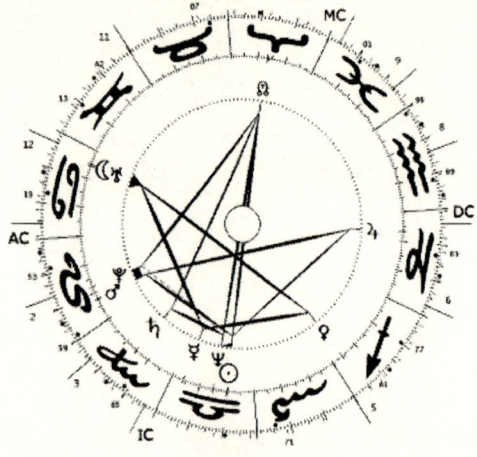

Shirley
13.10.1949, 23:30, Liverpool, UK

"My first thought was that it is like a star reaching out but also saying 'I'm here, look at me'. It seems open and unrestricted, reaching for the roof. Looking again there is a butterfly pinned down by its feet; I have sometimes felt restricted by home and environment."

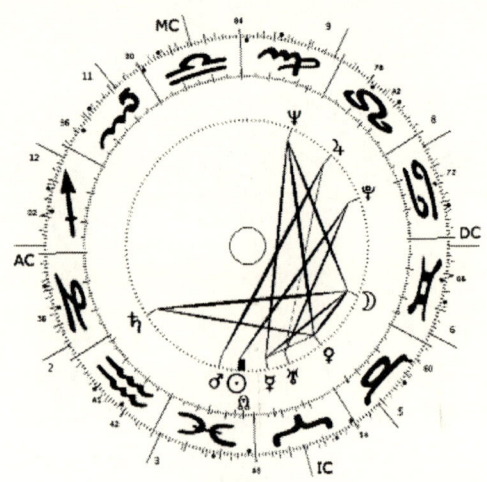

Jenny
14.03.1932, 02:00, Lahore, Pakistan

"The chart looks solid, impregnable, enclosed, safe, balanced. I like the feeling I get from it, but it feels stronger and more powerful and secure than I feel I appear and am. The picture is of an envelope filled with many things, or a Trojan horse."

The following example is a student's impressions of a chart they were working on. The student was asked to say what their intuitive response to the chart picture was, and what initial thoughts this gave them about the person.

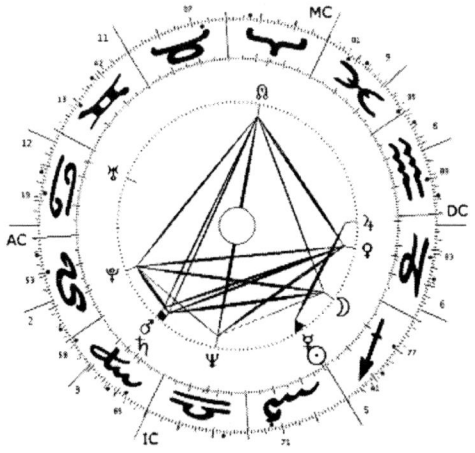

Stella
21.11.1949, 20:00, London, UK

"There are three images that spring to mind. The first is that of a pyramid, with a solid base, reaching up into the heavens. Or is it a tent that has an opening between the Moon and Venus, where one could step inside after having first negotiated the sextile (like a stile)? Because it is almost enclosed it gives a feeling of safety. I feel I would want to climb the tent pole which is fixed to the middle, to see what was at the top, perhaps to hang a light there to illuminate the whole tent. Alternatively, there seems to be a passage leading down under the floor to Neptune and hidden depths.

The second image is that of an enclosed trampoline. The base here is springy and allows movement. When one bounces on the trampoline the base gives slightly, propelling one upwards to almost touch the top. Unfortunately gravity dictates that one cannot stay there forever and down one comes. But perhaps with lots of practice, one can learn to reach higher and in doing so can touch the top more often.

The final image is that of a mountain. There are six ropes on the mountain and six different climbers attempting to scale its sides. Each of the climbers has a different approach and each is talented in his or her own way. They all have support from the base camps down below but each sets off from a different place, so has a different view of the task ahead. All the climbers are motivated in different ways to reach the top of the mountain and make their mark in the world.

The three images together make me feel that this chart is full of potential. It feels as though the chart (and the person it belongs to) is ever eager to rise upwards to new heights. Yet there is also a sense of containment, and a need to feel secure. The majority of the planets are in the bottom half of the chart, but the chart is also rising to the top so the upper half must be lived in too. The planets in the lower half seem to be where Stella would find the security she needs in order to feel safe enough to venture out into the larger world. In doing this she will have the safety net at the bottom to fall back on whenever she needs to.

Uranus is unconnected as there are no aspect lines flowing between it and the centre, so it is likely to be activated by the environment rather than having inner motivation."

In my work as a teacher and correspondence tutor for API(UK), I have used my own chart countless times to illustrate what I've been teaching, so as a final example I offer my thoughts on the visual images I see in my chart (opposite page).

The initial visual impact of my chart when I saw it drawn up in the Huber style for the first time was that it looked like a space capsule which has just blasted off from a launch pad (the Linear square aspects) and is in full flight on a journey to the Moon. The image of flight – fast, free and exciting – I relate to strongly. I like the 'space' flavour of the image a lot; in my own imagination and fantasy world I feel quite at home with the idea of space travel, and I love the vastness and beauty of the stars

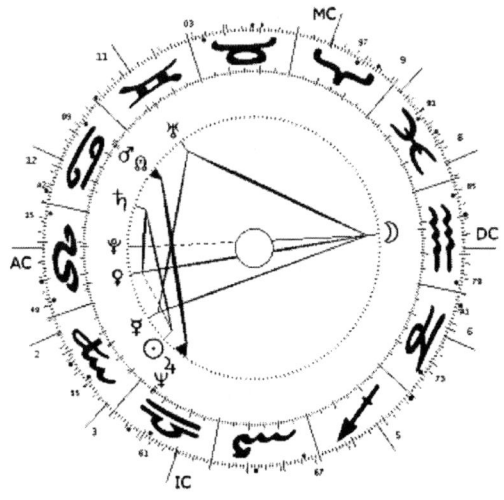

Joyce Hopewell
19.09.1945, 02:30, Tadcaster, UK

in the night sky. The Moon, on the sharp end of the space capsule, is both the destination and the journey. Standing out so prominently, it leads the rest of the chart into areas of discovery and the possibility of learning/sensing more. It can pick up the tangible and the intangible.

**Saturn 5 Moon Capsule
NASA, Houston, Texas**

The other image I see is also associated with speed, travel and fast, sometimes dangerous, movement. A fast, ocean-going racing yacht is plunging, racing and dipping through high waves. It is tipped on to its side, and its keel may even be temporarily below the water. Anyone on the yacht has to hang on tightly and provide weight in the right places to ensure the yacht wins the race. The sail – large, like a spinnaker – catches the wind and senses the way forward, with the Moon acting like a sensing pennant at the very top of the mast.

Exercise – Chart Image

Now it's over to you! On the next page are five charts, which will be your working charts for this section of the book. You will need to refer back them as you move through the exercises in this chapter. Each of them has a strong visual image which you are now invited to look for and speculate upon.

- Write down your intuitive response to each chart, noting the image or images that you see, and say what initial thoughts this gives you about the person. There are no right or wrong answers here – this is purely an exercise to encourage you to look at the whole aspect structure in each chart in a similar way to the examples already given.

- For the final stage of this particular exercise you are invited to take a look at your own chart, concentrating on the picture or pictures you see in your chart and relate this to your own life experience. Be honest and stay open to what comes up for you in this exercise. Then write some notes for yourself about the images you saw in your own chart, and what they mean for you.

If you are using other charts, maybe of friends or family, you can discuss with them what you see in their charts and ask for their feedback. This is the very best way to learn.

Birth Data for Working Charts

Chart A: 08.08.1952, 11:15 (10:15 GMT), 52.36 N, 02.05 W
Chart B: 14.01.1973, 18:30 GMT, 53.12.N, 02.53 W
Chart C: 08.12.1974, 20:30 GMT, 05.33 N, 00.13 W
Chart D: 03.05.1956, 05:30 (04:30 GMT), 53.25 N, 02.55 W
Chart E: 04.07.1946, 06:05 (05:05 GMT), 53.25 N, 02.55 W

2. Seeing the Whole Person 19

Working Charts

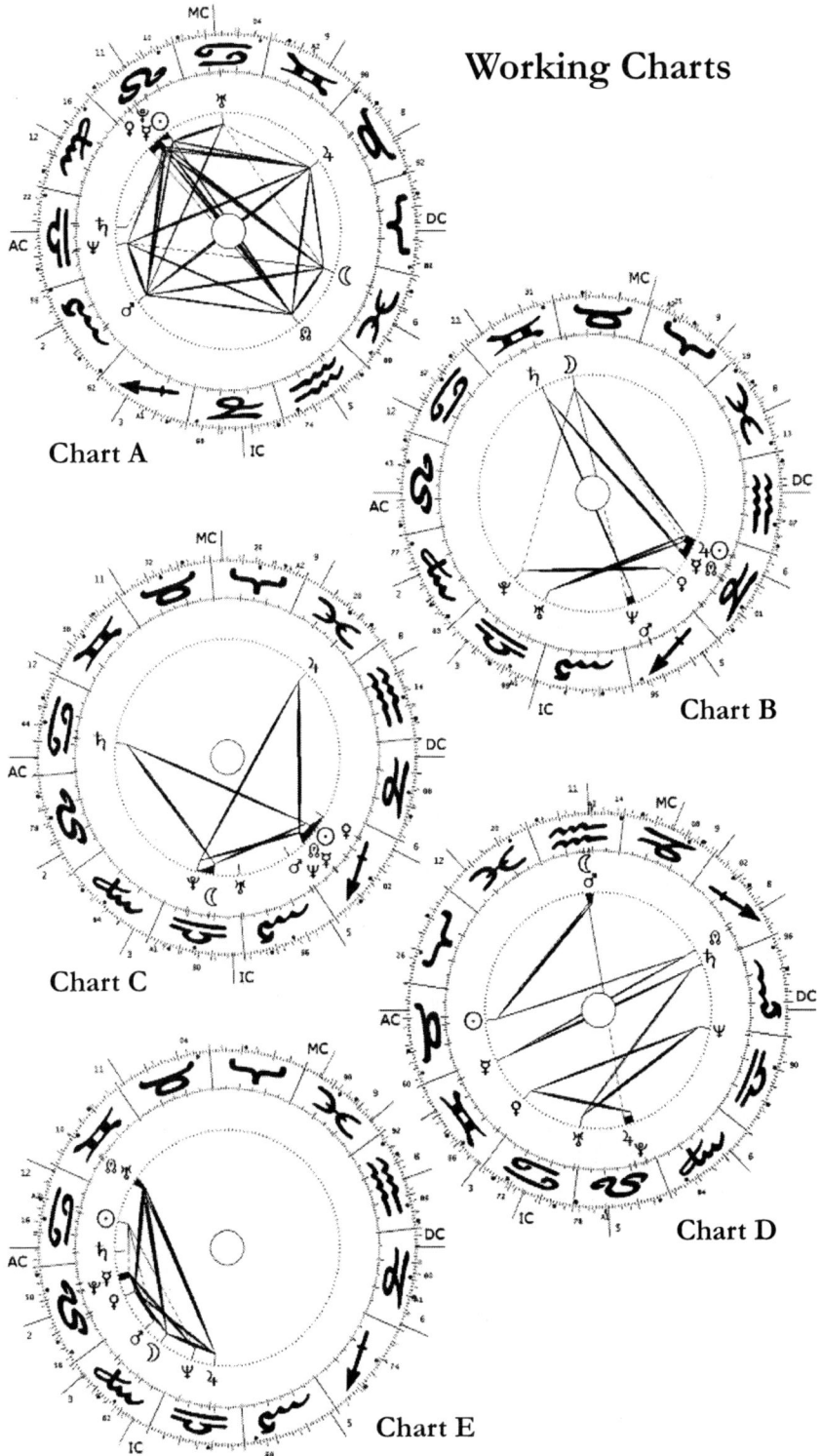

Chart A

Chart B

Chart C

Chart D

Chart E

Aspect Colours and Motivation

If you have your own chart set up in the Huber style you will be able to see it in full colour with the aspects spanning the chart shown in red, green and blue. Colour, as used in Huber charts, relates to specific qualities of energy and to the inner motivation which drives us to be, react and respond in certain ways. This is often unconscious, but if it can be understood, and we can bring it into consciousness, we can get a handle on it and work with it far more successfully. This will then have an impact on the way we live our lives.

The aspect colours and their qualities and significance are already covered in *The Cosmic Egg Timer*, so in this section we will be looking specifically at the influence the aspect colour balance in your own chart might have on your motivation – in short, what makes you tick!

If you have a lot of red aspects, which embody Cardinal energy, you will be an active, "doing" person. With a large number of blue aspects you will have a lot of Fixed energy, so will be content to "be", and hang on to things. If there are many green aspects, you will have plenty of Mutable energy, which will give you a tendency to be changeable, sensitive, and open to learning new things. There is an "ideal" ratio of 2 green : 4 red : 6 blue aspects to be taken into consideration, so rather than just count up the numbers of each aspect, you will need to see their overall balance in the context of this ratio.

For example, I have 3 green, 5 red, 2 blue aspects in my chart. That's a lot of red, a fair amount of green and very little blue. In terms of what drives me, and how I'm motivated to respond to life, it means I can be very busy and likely to always be on the go (excess red), I can be a bit touchy with plenty of nervous energy (high red/green balance) and I have to consciously remember to take time out and rest because just "being" is not uppermost in my priorities (lack of blue).

Exercise – Aspect Colours

Without looking at your chart, answer the following questions as honestly as you can, writing down your responses so that you can refer to them later:

1. How busy am I? Too busy... not busy enough... just right?

2. What aims/goals/targets do I have? What am I aiming to get done at the moment?

3. What stops or blocks me from doing things and using my energy? Is there anything that holds me back?

4. Where do I get my ideas from? Do they come from inside or outside stimuli, or a combination of these?

5. How well can I adapt to changing circumstances? Am I going through a time of change right now?

6. Do I have a long term view or vision of how I would like my life to be?....or how I would like to be?

7. Do I live in the present, the "here and now" enough? Can I seize the moment and enjoy it?

8. What gives me pleasure and enjoyment? Make a list of the things in life which provide pleasure, from the mundane to the exotic.

9. What stops me enjoying life? Is there anything that gets in the way?

Now look at your own chart and count up the number of aspects of each colour. If you have two aspects which are close together, and the planets making them are less than 4 degrees apart, you count just one, rather than two aspects. That is because aspects this close to each other are more likely to operate as one unit than as two separate aspects.

[Exercise continues on next page.]

> ### Exercise – Aspect Colours (continued)
>
> When you've worked out the colour balance in your own chart you'll have a good idea of the quality of energy which is uppermost, and this will affect your motivation; you may be an active, red "doing" person, a laid back, blue "being" person, or someone who is continually thinking, searching and questing – a green person. If you have a strong combination of two of these three colours, as I do with red and green, then these are likely to dominate your motivation. For example, I have a high red/green quotient which makes me responsive and reactive.
>
> - Now look at your responses to the questions you've just answered in the light of the colour balance in your chart and see how this fits in with your own life experiences. You may want to take some time to ponder on this and relate it back to significant periods or events in your life. Make some notes for yourself on your findings.
>
> ▫ ▫ ▫ ▫ ▫

"What if I have the 'ideal' balance of colour?"

Many people do have this, and they don't find any big imbalances in the way they experience their energies at work in everyday life. They have the capacity to use the motivating energies available to them in a balanced way, swapping from one mode to another comfortably, and as situations demand.

"What if I have an excess of blue aspects, but I'm always on the go?"

That would suggest that there is sufficient red energy/motivation to keep you going, to the extent that you live in the red, and forget that you have untapped resources within you to rest, relax, enjoy, stabilise and appreciate the fruits of your hard work. It's very easy to "live" in one colour and ignore the others.

"What about a chart that has all green/blue aspects, and only one red?"

The person with this kind of colour balance may simply delegate all the "doing" activities to someone else in their lives and be content to direct what goes on around them from the comfort of an armchair! Alternatively, they may try to compensate for their lack of red, working extremely hard to fulfil all their obligations and carry out all the tasks they need to, so the impression they give is of someone who is a workaholic, always busy doing something. But because they lack cardinal energy, they may experience burn out, get tired very quickly, or will simply never manage to complete what they set out to do, so it becomes a case of "work is always in progress."

Chart Shaping and Motivation

The overall shaping of the aspect structure in the chart is covered in *The Cosmic Egg Timer*. The chart shaping offers significant clues about motivation. The overall chart shaping can be Cardinal (aspect structure composed purely of linear aspect lines), Fixed (aspect figures of four or more sides) or Mutable (aspect figures of three sides).

Of course, it's not quite as simple and straightforward as that because some charts have a combination of two shapings – cardinal and mutable, cardinal and fixed, etc. For example, my own chart (page 17) has two triangular aspect figures and some disconnected aspect lines indicating that I am, for the most part, flexible and adaptable. But sometimes I get very restless, and this is when the cardinal, linear aspects are at work.

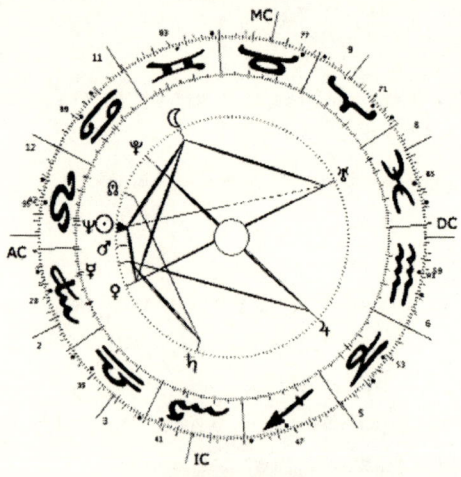

Richard
14.08.1925, 06:19, Sidcup, UK

The shaping in Richard's chart is a combination of fixed and cardinal. There is a four-sided figure which is bisected by a zig-zagging disconnected line. This person describes themselves as someone who has a life pattern of needing security, so they would found or set up a business or organisation. This would become established, but then the need to make changes or create something new would kick in. What had been set up was then either dismantled, sold on, or abandoned as the linear pattern – often a very creative one – came into play, making way for something new.

Exercise – Chart Shaping

Take a look at your own chart now, and assess it's overall shaping/motivation. How does this relate to what you already know about yourself? Be honest about this, and make some notes on your findings.

- Using the five working charts from page 19, decide which is the dominant shaping in each, making notes on each chart as you do this. Remember, though, that some charts have a combination of two shapings.

Answers are on page 46.

Chart Direction and Motivation

The direction in which the aspect structure in the chart is oriented is another factor to take into consideration when assessing the unconscious, inner motivation of an individual. Does the chart have a Vertical or a Horizontal orientation?

If it's vertical, the direction of movement is from the IC to the MC, and this suggests a motivation to move and grow upwards. A vertical chart indicates an individualiser, someone who wants to get ahead, to reach the MC at the highest point of the chart. They will be a ladder-climber, achiever, high flier and will seek to stand out in the crowd and be noticed. People with vertical charts can, on the whole, stand alone easily. They are not afraid to put their head above the parapet; they will seek to get on in life and to be recognised for what they have achieved. The downside is that they may neglect personal relationships in order to do this, so although they have the ability to scale the heights, their achievements could be accompanied by a sense of isolation. It's important to consider also that the upward direction and urge to grow and develop in this way might also follow the path of emotional, mental and spiritual growth; as well as the drive to achieve it may denote an urge to grow towards the light and reach the metaphorical mountain top.

If the chart has a horizontal direction – from the AC to the DC (left to right) – this indicates someone who seeks contact, and who wants or needs to work, interact, or simply be with others. They may not cope easily without people around them, and they are unlikely to go it alone. They are less interested in individualising and are therefore less competitive in this sphere. A person with a horizontal chart will want to be involved with their surroundings, and the area where they may be competitive is in relationships.

It's important to acknowledge that we might make compromises between the motivations indicated by these two directions. We can become controlled by our surroundings on the horizontal axis, and we may become isolated and suffer misunderstandings on the vertical axis.

26   *The Living Birth Chart*

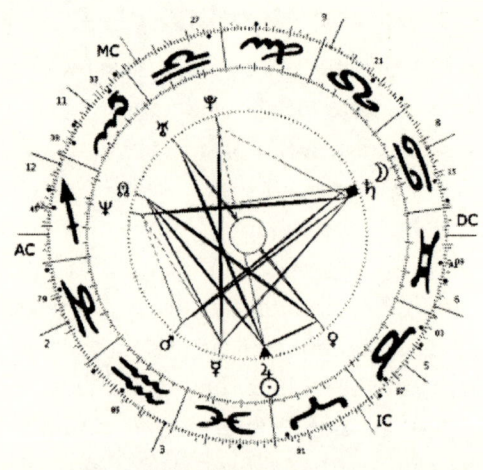

Alwyn
22.03.1975, 03:00, Cardiff, UK

Sometimes, as in the example above, a chart will not fall clearly into either category and will appear to have aspects moving in both directions. This indicates that the person will be able to switch modes, and will be equally comfortable with others as they will with asserting their own individuality.

Exercise – Chart Direction

- Take a look at your own chart once again, and assess it's overall direction/motivation. How does this relate to what you already know about yourself? Being as honest as you can about this, make some notes on your findings.

- Using the 5 working charts from page 19, assess the direction of each, making notes for yourself, and bear in mind that some charts may show both directions and therefore both motivations.

Answers are on page 46.

If you are working with the charts of friends and family, or if you are already taking tentative steps to try out what you're learning with other charts set up in the Huber style, it's important to be as fully aware as you can of where **you** are coming from when you discuss a chart. In view of this, we are taking the topic of direction one stage further: if you have a vertical chart, beware! You may look down on your clients without even realising it. And if you have a horizontal chart, you may get too involved with them and what they want and demand from you. In this situation, it would be all-too-easy to end up telling them what they want to hear, so we need to be aware of not being controlled by our clients by receiving praise which feeds the ego.

Exercise – Chart Direction and Motivation

Write down as many different words, phrases or descriptions as you can, in non-astrological terms, to describe the motivation associated with a vertical and a horizontal chart direction. Imagine you have to explain to someone who knows no astrology what you can see in their chart in terms of its direction, and that you are trying to get them to talk about it with you.

For example, you might say:

- "It looks to me as though you are a person who aims to stand up and be counted in some way."
- "I get the impression from your chart that you like your achievements to be acknowledged."
- "It looks to me as if you are seeking recognition of some kind."
- "How is it for you to spend time alone?"
- "It looks like relationships are pretty important for you."

Public or Private? – "I" and "You" Sided Charts

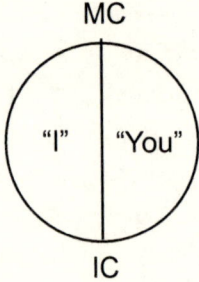

The meridian axis of the chart, marked by the IC and MC, divides our inner and outer worlds. Privacy and the need to spend time alone on the AC side of the chart begins at the meridian, so in addition to taking into consideration the steps in chart interpretation outlined so far, it's useful to assess whether the person, according to their chart, is likely to be a "public" or a "private" individual. If they are "public" they are going to be focussed on being with others and interacting with them; if they are "private" they are more comfortable in their own space and prefer to be alone; other people come in by invitation only.

"How can you see this?"

It's simple. You count up the number of planets either side of the meridian line in order to find which half of the chart has the most. The Moon's Node is not included in this count. The planets represent our psychological drives and if the majority of them are on the right of the meridian they are in the "public" sphere. The person has what we call a "You" sided chart because their orientation is towards contact with others. A larger number of planets on the left of the meridian are in the "private" area of the chart, giving that person an "I" sided chart which suggests they need their own space and are not so strongly motivated to make contact with others.

Planets on the "You" side of the chart are geared towards interacting and coping with the surroundings. The nature of any planet on the right hand side of the chart is to be open and involved in contact with others; if you have a "You" sided chart and try to withdraw from this contact then problems may arise. Planets on the "You" side of the chart are equipped to handle the stuff of others – their hurt, their pain and their problems, and are able to cope, even when things get tough.

Planets on the "I" side of the chart react very differently. On the left of the meridian is our inner space and sanctum, and this can feel violated if demands are put upon us without our consent. This is an area of self-protection and privacy where we won't want to readily reveal things about ourselves. Planets here are much more vulnerable, and if they feel "invaded" and overwhelmed by the demands and expectations of the surroundings, the person may suffer or feel very uncomfortable. Planets on this side of the chart are less well equipped to cope with hurt.

"What if you have planets at the top or bottom of the chart?"

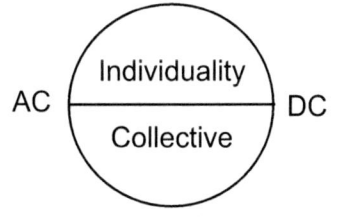

```
         Individuality
  AC  ┤               ├  DC
          Collective
```

Planets near the IC, in the lower half of the chart, can help us to connect strongly with our roots, family, home sphere or neighbourhood. They make us feel as if we really belong and are rooted comfortably here. We may use these planets to gain access to collective ideas, thoughts, feelings and viewpoints and they will enable us to work or participate in some way in the affairs of the community.

Planets near the MC will act as aspiration points for us to grow towards. They will help us to aim for the qualities that our highest planet represents, and they may be the tools we use to help us shine out in the world, attract attention or set the scene for how we express our individuality.

> **Exercise – Chart Hemispheres**
>
> - Using your own chart, count up the number of planets (excluding the Moon's Node) on either side of the meridian. The side with the greatest number of planets is the one that will be emphasised. Are you an "I" or a "You" sided person? Public or private? And how does this relate to what you already know about yourself?
>
> - Using the 5 working charts from page 19, assess each one, making notes for yourself, and say whether it is "I" or "You" sided, and if there are planets around the IC or MC.
>
> *Answers are on page 46.*

"What if there are large open spaces in the chart, like in Chart E where the aspects are all bunched closely together?"

Some charts will have this feature; there will be an open space with no aspects which will leave the central core of the chart exposed. Refer back to Chart E, and to the charts of Eric and Shirley on pages 13 and 14.

Chart E has no aspects to the right of the trine between Jupiter and Uranus/Node, leaving the "You" side and most of the upper hemisphere of the chart open and exposed to the environment. There is nothing to stop whatever comes from the outside world from reaching the "I" side of this woman's chart, which is where she will feel safest. Because there are no aspects traversing these parts of the chart it's as if there are no hurdles to be vaulted or barriers to be crossed, so this person will feel that others invade her privacy far too fast for her liking and comfort. This will make her feel vulnerable, maybe uneasy, and possibly shy. She may feel as if it is "open season" as far as meeting others and making her own mark on the world is concerned; she may easily become overwhelmed and move further away into the comfort of the "I" side of her chart.

Eric's chart also has its central core open to the "You" side, but the open space here is much smaller. He will still have feelings of vulnerability when first meeting people, and may hold back at first, but with Moon and Venus as the two planets closest to the DC, what people will pick up on will be the gentle and sensitive qualities of these planets.

Shirley's chart has a similarly narrower open space towards the "You" side, focussed on the 3rd quadrant of the chart which is associated with the **conscious** "You" area of interaction. She may compensate for any vulnerability here with her Jupiter placed strongly just before the DC, welcoming all-comers with friendly optimism and a warm sense of humour.

If there is an open space in the lower hemisphere of a chart with most of the planets in the upper half, the person can feel vulnerable within the collective and will seek to get away from the ideas and types of interaction found there. With an open space on the "I" side, and the majority of planets on the "You" side of the chart, the individual will tend to seek out the company of others and their personal inner space and privacy is likely to be a no-go area for them because there is nothing to draw them towards this.

Aspect Patterns

Having looked at some of the initial techniques involved in working with the chart as a whole, we now move on to the aspects and their patterns.

Aspect Pattern Astrology is unique to the Huber approach. Many aspect patterns were first recognised and developed by Bruno Huber, based on his empirical research into the charts and real life experiences of the clients and ordinary people whose charts he studied. Over 45 distinct aspect patterns are recognised in the Huber method, and they relate to motivation which comes from the deepest inner level of the chart, where energy and motivation is often unconscious. The whole chart picture which we have already looked at is composed of different, individual aspect patterns. Patterns are quadrangular or triangular in shaping and motivation, and their motivation corresponds to fixed qualities (quadrangular shapes) and mutable qualities (triangular shapes). There can also be disconnected, incomplete aspect lines which do not come together to form either a three or a four (or more) sided figure. These are known as linear or incomplete patterns and their motivation is cardinal. The colour or colours of aspect lines present in each individual aspect pattern is significant, and similar guidelines apply to the aspect colours as those already outlined. Each pattern is made up of one, two or three colours – red, blue and green.

Whereas in more conventional approaches to astrology it is usual to look at a planet and then interpret it in some detail against the zodiac sign that it's in, with the Huber method more emphasis is laid upon the interrelationship **between** the planets, and the recognisable patterns that these connections form. The patterns the aspects make are indicators of motivation, and are of primary importance because they allow us to see how the person "ticks".

The aspect patterns operate at the level of unconscious motivation in the chart. If we can bring these behavioural patterns into consciousness and become more aware of how they operate and manifest in everyday behaviour, we can begin to use them more effectively and productively because we will understand how they operate. This awareness and understanding is both enriching and enlightening. On a personal level, it can help us focus and keep on track as opposed to getting bogged down and lost along the way.

"How do aspect patterns work?"

In *The Cosmic Egg Timer* I described a selection of common aspect patterns and how they operate. Here I give another four with illustrative charts.

The Ambivalence Triangle

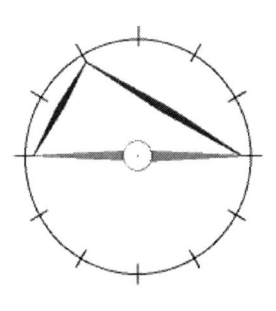

This figure is frequently found in charts. It is triangular, so has a mutable motivation, making it work in a flexible way, adapting to change as necessary. But it's made up of red and blue aspects with no green aspects involved, which gives it a "black and white" way of operating as it uses the red aspect to get active and "do", and the blue aspects to enjoy life and just "be". In the Ambivalence figure, the red working energy is held in tension in the opposition aspect, and much working energy is used here. The more relaxed blue energy in this pattern has a focal point where the two blue aspects meet. The planet here is sometimes called the "escape" planet as the person will use and express the qualities of this planet when they switch off from work, relax and enjoy themselves. The ambivalence in the name for this aspect pattern refers to its work/rest cycle of behaviour. People with this pattern are pulled between two opposing forces – doing and being (the effect of the red and blue aspects). They might be getting on with the job in hand and putting a lot of effort into it, yet all the while they yearn for some rest and relaxation, looking with longing at whatever the blue "escape" planet represents for them in their lives. When they have completed their work tasks and take some time out, they will enjoy this for a while, but when that niggling feeling comes along that they really ought to be **doing** something, or that it's time to get back to work, they flip right back into red, working mode. Then the whole cycle repeats itself again.

Each aspect pattern will be modified and influenced by the planets involved, so this always needs to be held in mind when looking at aspect patterns in individual charts. The whole chart has to be taken into consideration, using all the factors we've covered so far.

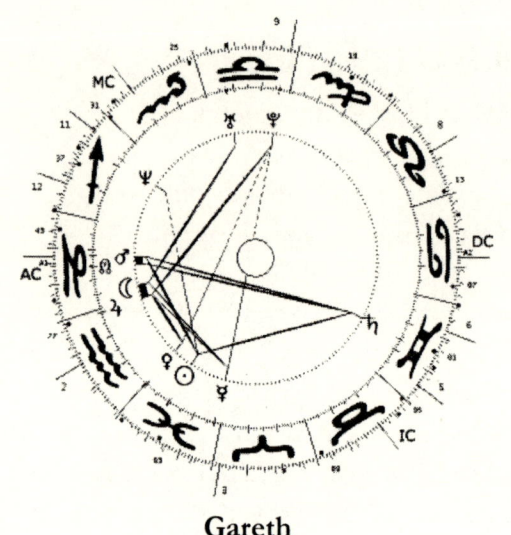

Gareth
01.03.1973, 04:45, Crewe, UK

In Gareth's chart, there is an Ambivalence triangle, pinned by Mercury opposite Pluto, with Jupiter in the blue corner as the "escape" planet. The conjunction of Moon with Jupiter perhaps emphasises the need to escape. One visual image we might see in the chart is of the head of a comical cartoon figure, rather like the "Road Runner" rooster, with its wide open mouth or beak pointing towards the "You". We might also see a flower which is opening up with the tips of its petals reaching towards the "You" side of the chart. Note also that there is considerable vulnerability here as these images show the central core of the chart exposed to the "You" with no aspects to protect it. There are more planets on the "I" side of the chart, so Gareth will not like feeling "invaded" or overwhelmed on first meeting new people. There is a strong focus of planets around the AC and in the 1st house, suggesting he will be more of a private person, and will need time to himself. The planets people first contact on meeting him are Saturn and Pluto on the "You" side; he might be a little cautious and reserved at first, and he doesn't suffer fools gladly. The direction is mainly vertical, and the chart shaping is triangular, with some linear aspects. He is flexible and adaptable, as the predominantly mutable motivation suggests, with a touch of restlessness. He has 4 red, 4 green and 5 blue aspects, so there's quite a lot of sensitivity and nervous energy to expend and he may not always get enough time to relax and "be". Gareth says:

> *"This seems basically right. The only thing I wasn't so sure about here was being so flexible and adaptable. I don't think I am always that way – I can be quite stubborn."*

Gareth works in research, using Mercury and Pluto in the red opposition part of the Ambivalence triangle. With these he gathers the facts and analyses the data he needs to produce reports on various topics. He currently works as a researcher in the energy sector, has researched health care, and for many years prior to this he was undertaking intensive research for his PhD. Both Mercury and Pluto are psychologically on the 3/9 Thought axis, reflecting the nature of the work they are applied to and emphasising the theme of thinking and ideas. Periods of intense work involving gathering facts, studying and analysing them have always been interspersed with the need to get away and travel.

With Jupiter as the blue "escape" planet he has often chosen adventurous activities and solo trips as an independent traveller. Gareth has long had a taste for hot-air ballooning, gliding, flying lessons, fast cars and routes less travelled. Jupiter as the blue "escape" planet in this pattern is conjunct the Moon, suggesting that he gets a lot of enjoyment and fun in his time off, which balances out the intense work and mental concentration involved in the red aspect in this pattern.

> *"Yes I do like to escape, but I don't see it just as escaping, it's also about making the most of the opportunities to get more out of life. I like to have the escapes from work, which in part act as motivation to get the work done. Either when work is too busy, or boring, it's nice to have the thought of having an escape route – mostly through having the next holiday booked."*

The Trampoline

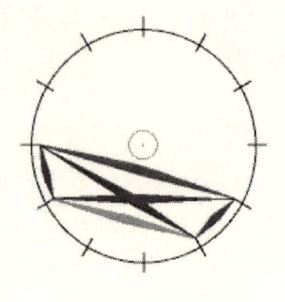

This figure is found less frequently in charts, but is usually significant in the charts of individuals where it is present. The shape is quadrangular, giving a Fixed motivation which seeks stability and security. All three colours are present in a combination of 3 green aspects, 2 blue and 1 red. These bring cardinal, fixed and mutable energy to this figure, with an emphasis on green, mutable energy. Although this is a fixed figure, it is likely to operate with considerable flexibility because of the green aspects. These are visually evident as they make up most of the outside of the figure (a quincunx and 2 semi-sextiles), and form the bouncy, flexible membrane which fits on the frame of the Trampoline. This outer membrane gives the impression of someone who is flexible, sensitive, perceptive and versatile in their thinking. There is a sense of inner stability and strength which comes from the fixed trines on the inside, which are like the supporting struts in the Trampoline's framework. This inner stability suggests that there are likely to be high inner ideals. People with this figure are more likely to be focussed on what is going on inside and may give the impression of not always having time for those around them. They will generally be easy-going and not aggressive. However, if they feel they're getting pushed around, they are quite capable of pushing back, drawing on the cardinal energy of the underlying square. The ability to push back will be determined by the qualities of the pinning planets.

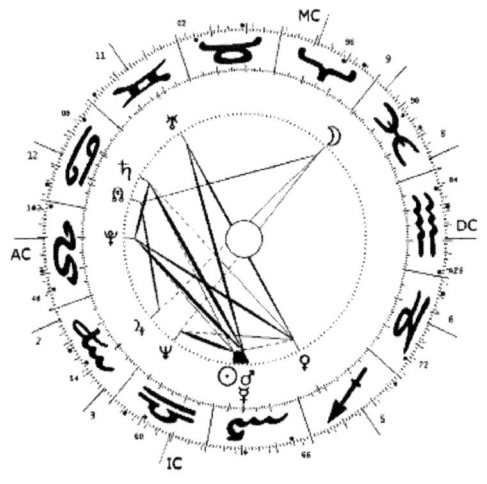

Eric
28.10.1944, 23:45, Lincoln, UK

Eric's chart has a Trampoline which is pinned by Sun, Venus, Saturn and Pluto. The figure spans houses 12 to 4 on the "I" side of this chart, which has a visual image reminiscent of a sailing boat with Moon on top of the mast, Uranus at the prow and a large spinnaker sail billowing in the wind.

This chart also has an exposed central core, again suggesting vulnerability, but Moon and Venus on the "You" side as the first planets met gives a sense of softness. The chart shaping shows a mixture of fixed and mutable motivation, indicating that Eric can operate in both modes. The direction is vertical with a colour balance of 5 red, 5 green and 6 blue. The comparatively high ratio of green aspects suggest that Eric will prefer to think, reflect and generate new ideas.

The majority of the planets involved in Eric's Trampoline are strong rather than gentle in nature and expression, and it's worth noting that his Sun, which is conjunct Mercury and Mars, is intercepted, so it will seek output via the other planets that it aspects, namely most of those involved in the Trampoline.

Eric is a quiet but easy-going and friendly person who seldom raises his voice or loses his temper. But on the occasions when he has felt pushed around or put upon, the Trampoline has pushed back with dramatic and unexpected effect. He speaks of being quiet and well-behaved at school, keen to learn and rarely in trouble. But when he was picked on by a bully, the combination of Saturn, Pluto and his Scorpio Sun/Mars in this figure was startling and decisive. The bully received an unexpected bloody nose and never bothered him again.

The Recorder

This is a quadrangular figure composed of all three aspect colours. Fixed in motivation, it can utilise the one red aspect to manifest the imaginative capacity of the blue and green aspects. As this pattern has as its components a Search figure, a Small Talent triangle and two Small Learning triangles, it contains and presents many possibilities.

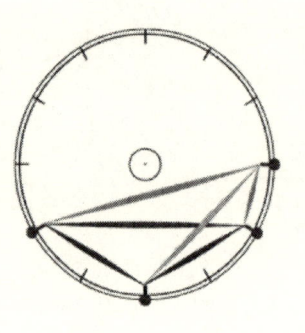

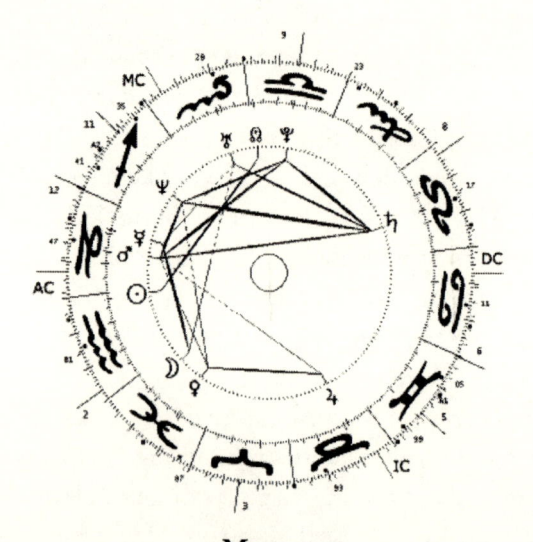

May
22.1.1977, 08:15, Amiens, France

May is an art historian who is at the time of writing working in a museum, researching and cataloguing paintings. Here, she offers some feedback on how she experiences the Recorder at work in her own life, as well as adding additional comments to what I've suggested about her chart. I told her that the Recorder has a huge storage capacity and that it is able to record what is observed in the environment. The Hubers describe it as functioning like a recorder which *"stores, among other things, feelings, situations and destinies, and can replay them in such a way that one imagines they are there."* The red/green planet (Mars) acts as the observer in this pattern and its role is critical to the overall ability to record and store. May says:

> *"Yes I agree with this, I can remember things very clearly and have an excellent visual memory. I look around a lot, and can recall a lot of what I see. I can also replay feelings and situations easily."*

May's chart looks like an open mouth, eager to taste and take things in, and it's also like a protective visor, ready to slam shut at the first hint of danger.

> *"Yes, that's right. I like new things, new places, I want to try new experiences, and you can ask the husband about my 'slamming shut' if I'm not happy!"*

The chart is "I" sided, with both fixed and mutable motivation, giving May the ability to adapt and adjust as well as wanting to stick with what works. The direction of the aspect structure is predominantly horizontal, so even though the "You" side of the chart is exposed, May will be willing to make contact with others. She has a colour balance of 4 red, 2 green and 9 blue aspects, the excess blue supporting and emphasising her need for security and also suggesting that she finds it very easy to relax and just "be".

> *"Yes I do need to feel safe, but have to say I don't find it that easy to relax all the time."*

May's chart shows the potential for considerable talent which is embedded within the three Small Talent triangles she has:

one in the lower, unconscious, hemisphere of the chart pinned by Mars, Venus and Jupiter, one spanning Houses 2-9 pinned by Moon, Mercury and Uranus and the other in the upper, conscious, hemisphere pinned by Saturn, Neptune and Pluto. The presence of a Small Talent triangle in a chart suggests the person has a still-developing talent or ability. This is inherent potential waiting to unfold and be expressed, but it has to be consciously worked at so that the development of the talent is ongoing throughout the whole lifetime. One of May's talents is connected to photography and the use of image. She is a keen photographer and many of her photographs have a special "something" about them, drawing the viewer in and touching something within which can evoke a powerful response. This can be related to the presence of both Neptune and Saturn in the upper Talent triangle.

> *"Well I do try to put something a bit 'different' into my photographs..."*

Saturn helps to practically "ground" and manifest the images, sights, views, faces and scenes that she sees and photographs. She drew on Saturnian practicality, too, when she learned to develop them herself, buying her own equipment to use at home – all this long before digital cameras came along!

But look closely and you will see that this upper hemisphere Talent triangle does not stand alone; it is part of the larger Recorder figure. The Recorder works in its own unique way, the component parts of this whole larger aspect pattern contributing to its overall mode of action.

What is interesting is that the Small Talent triangle in the lower half of the chart links directly in to the Recorder, via Mars in Capricorn in the 12th house. Mars is the red/green planet, the driving force which energises the Recorder. It acts as a fulcrum, activating both the upper and lower aspect patterns, and appears as the possible moving force not only in animating the talent embedded within her chart, but also as the impetus for the open mouth image.

The Dominant Learning Triangle

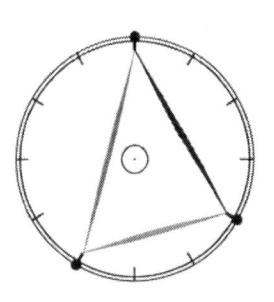

This large triangular figure has a mutable motivation, enabling it to go with the flow of life. It encompasses the central core of the chart and covers a lot of space in the aspect area of the chart. For those individuals in whose charts this pattern is found, a correspondingly large area of life experience is usually involved. The Dominant Learning triangle represents an ongoing sequence of learning which is likely to be a significant feature in the person's life. The learning process is one of growth, change and movement. Lessons which dominate the person's life will come up time and time again, and through these they will learn more about themselves and their interactions with others. The ongoing learning experience will help to hone and refine their own skills.

All three aspect colours are present in this pattern: the cardinal red square, the mutable green quincunx and the fixed blue trine. These give the ability to take action using the red aspect, to be aware, question, doubt and search using the green aspect and enjoy the fruits of labour in the blue aspect.

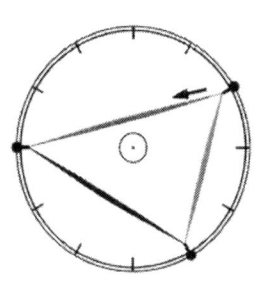

The direction the process of learning involved in this figure takes is important. Moving in an anti-clockwise direction, it always begins with the planet at the red/blue corner, where the square and trine meet. It moves along the quincunx and then returns along the trine to the place where it started. This gives a sequence of red-green-blue, and if the Dominant Learning triangle follows this sequence it is known as 'direct'. This is significant. A direct learning triangle suggests that the lessons can be learned and absorbed in a straightforward and uncomplicated way; life's lessons are learned quickly when this figure has a direct motion.

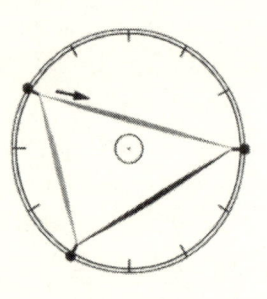

If the sequence follows a clockwise direction, the triangle is known as 'retrograde', since the sequence is reversed and becomes red-blue-green. The person will most probably find that they don't learn or completely understand the lessons that life presents the first time around, so they will go through the learning process a number of times before the penny drops and the learning process is complete.

If we find one of these learning triangles in a chart it's no good expecting the person to have just one specific lesson to learn. Life has a knack of presenting the same or similar lessons in different guises, so each time it does, the sequence described will be triggered.

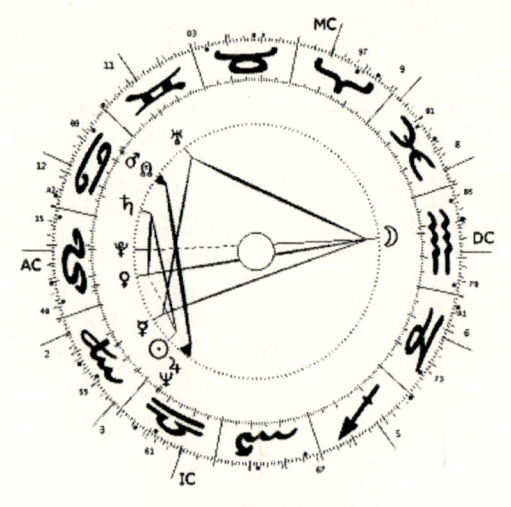

Joyce Hopewell
19.09.1945, 02:30, Tadcaster, UK

I use my own chart here to give an example of a direct Dominant Learning triangle at work, and my experience of this. I have already talked about my chart image, colour balance and shaping/motivation. My chart is horizontal; the Moon reaches out from the other planets on the "I" side to make contact with the "You", standing alone near the DC. It is the tension ruler in the chart, a focal point, and its energies are what others often pick up on when first meeting me (or so I've been told.)

The Dominant Learning triangle dominates the whole chart, as there are only two complete aspects patterns there. The planet at the starting point of the learning sequence is Uranus. A dissatisfaction with something will crop up – maybe I'm looking for some changes, suddenly noticing that things have become static and stale and need refreshing. Perhaps some inspirational ideas will come to me, demanding attention. I'll start thinking "There's got to be a new way or another way of doing this," and I'll suddenly become full of ideas, open to fresh input and new ways of looking at things associated with the situation that feels stale.

A lot of energy is expended at this point between Uranus, with its urge to make changes, and Mercury. I do some research, discuss what is possible and gather as much information as I can. The red, cardinal phase of the sequence having been completed, there is then a period of searching and seeking, and this is when the quincunx comes into play. I try out alternative ways of implementing my ideas. This is not always easy and there may be periods of trial and error as I try to find a way to make things work. Mercury amasses information and puts things through a testing phase, and with the 7th house Moon involved, I need to find out how it all "feels". Does it feel right, not just for me, but for others that I come into contact with. The Moon is fully engaged here, checking out the responses of others against my own. Once this feedback is in place, the ideas are put into practise and the changes are made. At this stage of the process, I can relax into the trine and enjoy the experience of something new made manifest.

Exercise – Aspect Patterns

Now it's over to you again, this time with an invitation to choose an aspect pattern from your own chart that you would like to know more about, or explore in greater depth. Once you've done that, refer back to the basic guidelines on how to work with aspect patterns, which are given in the introductory pages of the book, as these will help you as you approach this exercise.

Note the pinning planets in your aspect pattern and draw each of the glyphs on a separate piece of A5 sized paper – one for each planet.

You will need to clear some floor space – enough to be able to walk around comfortably without bumping into anything. You will also need some lengths of wool or coloured ribbons in the appropriate colours for your pattern. Lay these out on the floor in the shape of the aspect pattern you have chosen to work on, and lay the glyphs you have drawn at the correct corners of the laid-out aspect pattern.

When you have done this, stand in the middle of the space created by your aspect pattern on the floor, and take some time to consider the whole pattern with the pinning planets in place. What is its overall shaping and motivation? How does it work?

Look at the pinning planets and think about how they work and interact with each other, via the aspects that connect them. Do the planets, which each represent a psychological drive within yourself, have an easy-going relationship? Or are they in a challenging relationship? Look at the colours of aspects that the planets receive – this will tell you how the planets are lit up, and what quality of energy lights them.

[Exercise continues on next page.]

Exercise – Aspect Patterns (continued)

Walk around the outside of your laid-out aspect pattern, standing at the place of each of the pinning planets in turn. Look at the qualities of the other planets you connect with; be aware of the colours of aspects you give and receive, and how these will influence the way you interact with them.

As you stand in the place of each planet in turn, allow yourself to take on the shape, stance and qualities of this planet, and if you want to, you could begin a dialogue with one or more of the planets in the pattern. Maybe you could ask them why they're not as cooperative as they might be if you feel this pattern is not working for you as well as you'd like it to. Or you could ask them what they want from you, and tell them what you have to offer them. Of course, you'll have to move around the aspect pattern taking on these different roles of each of the planets yourself, but as each of them represents a drive within yourself, you could find this a useful and illuminating way of working with your aspect patterns. It will help you to understand them better and it will give you the opportunity to engage different aspects of yourself.

When you have finished this exercise (you'll know when is the right time to stop), make a few notes for yourself about what you have discovered. You might find it helpful to keep a loose-leaf folder or notebook on your astrological work on aspect patterns, planets and many of the other Huber techniques we'll be looking at in this book, so you can ground your experience of each one by making a few notes as an important final stage in each exercise.

¤ ¤ ¤ ¤ ¤

Answers to Exercises on Example Charts

Page 24, Chart Shaping:
Chart A - Fixed;
Chart B - Cardinal
Chart C - Mutable
Chart D - Cardinal
Chart E - Fixed/Mutable

Page 26, Chart Direction:
Chart A – Vertical
Chart B – Vertical
Chart C – Vertical
Chart D – Vertical and Horizontal
Chart E – Vertical

Page 30, Chart Hemispheres:
Chart A – "I" sided; Uranus on MC
Chart B – "You" sided; majority of planets in lower hemisphere
Chart C – "You" sided; majority of planets in lower hemisphere
Chart D – Equally "I" and "You" sided; more planets in lower hemisphere
Chart E – "I" sided; Jupiter and Neptune near IC

Chapter 3

Integrating the Personality

The Threefold Personality – The Ego Planets

The planets represent our psychological drives. In the birth chart, the planets are placed on the interface between the aspects which infuse them with energy of a specific kind, depending on the aspects involved, and the signs and houses they are in. The signs determine which characteristics and traits they might assume and the houses show in which area of life their expression and interaction with the environment will take place.

In the Huber Method of astrological psychology, we group the planets into three distinct categories:

- Tool Planets – Mercury ☿, Venus ♀, Mars ♂, Jupiter ♃
- Ego Planets – Sun ☉, Moon ☽, Saturn ♄
- Transpersonal Planets – Uranus ♅, Neptune ♆, Pluto ♇

The Tool planets represent our drives to survive, keep ourselves safe and have a sense of well-being. They fulfil basic needs which have to be met before we can begin to grow in consciousness and function in a more "awake" manner. Tool planets often function at a subconscious level, supporting our fundamental survival needs.

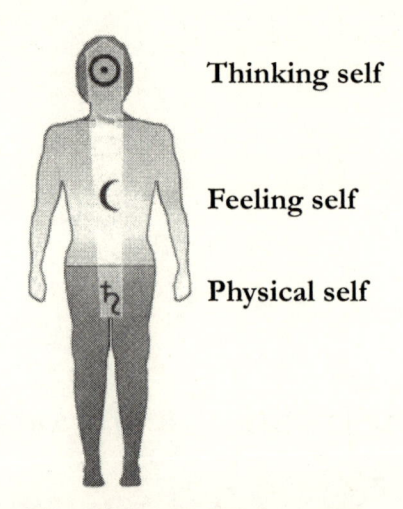

The Threefold Personality

- Thinking self
- Feeling self
- Physical self

The Ego planets represent the drives and energies associated with the physical, emotional and mental self – our body, feelings and mind. We identify strongly with these aspects of self and live out much of our daily lives through them. Ego planets have the potential to be used consciously, and if we are on the path of personal and spiritual growth, it's up to us to develop, fine-tune and integrate those parts of ourselves represented by these planets.

The Transpersonal planets represent higher qualities which we might aspire to, but which we tend to forget about in our more personality-oriented lives. The qualities and energies of the transpersonal planets have to be consciously cultivated and developed so that they can be used for the benefit of humanity, rather than just for our personal selves.

In this chapter we will be looking in depth at the ego planets – Sun, Moon and Saturn – which represent our body, feelings and mind/will. The Sun represents our sense of self through the mind and use of the personal will, the Moon our sense of self through the feelings and Saturn our sense of self through the body. Included are some practical exercises to help you familiarise yourself with how these planets might function in your own life, with suggestions on how to develop them and bring them more fully into consciousness. At the end of the chapter are suggestions on which features to consider when looking at the placement and positioning of the ego planets in your own chart. Before you embark upon any of the practical exercises in this chapter, it will be useful to note where your own Sun, Moon and Saturn are positioned.

Position of Sun, Moon and Saturn

☉ **The Sun** is ideally positioned somewhere in the upper hemisphere of the chart where it can shine and be seen. When it is here we can more easily express qualities of leadership, goal-oriented behaviour and the drive to become an autonomous individual, especially if the Sun is on the MC or in the 10th house. Positioned in the lower hemisphere, the Sun will not shine so readily or be seen to shine: the individual has to work harder at asserting themselves and gaining recognition. Placed on or near the AC, the Sun tends to express itself differently. It may be more secretive, private and shy, reluctant to broadcast achievements and blow its own trumpet if it is in the 12th house. This could change if it is in the 1st house, where there is a strong sense of "me first". On the DC it will be more accessible and assertive as it is readily available to meet others and can push itself towards them with confidence and a sense of purpose. This will be far easier if the Sun is above the DC; if it's just below the DC this could demand greater effort.

☽ **The Moon** is ideally placed somewhere on the horizontal I/You axis of the chart where it enables the person to readily make contact with others, allowing them to experience the "You" as a mirror and express emotional needs. If the Moon is on the horizontal axis, but on the AC side of the chart in the 12th house, the individual will need privacy and space, and will be less inclined to actively make contact. If the Moon is found near the DC, in the 6th or 7th house, it is accessible but may also be vulnerable because it will pick up feelings from the "You" very easily. Moon in the lower hemisphere, especially near the IC and the bottom of the chart may feel comfortably "ordinary" in the collective and relish home comforts; in the upper hemisphere and near the MC Moon will feel very visible and will require praise and acknowledgement for any achievements.

♄ Saturn is ideally placed in the lower hemisphere of the chart, below the horizon. Here it can provide a psychological safe base, rather like a secure safety net which can break falls and provide support if needed, or a solid rock offering structure and form. Saturn in the 4th house or close to the IC would have this effect, like a tree with strong roots anchoring us to a place of safety within the collective. Saturn high up in the chart near the MC can be likened to a tree growing up in the air with its dangling roots exposed and not grounded in the earth. If Saturn is positioned above the horizon, we may experience some insecurities. If Saturn is on the AC side of the chart we may be a private, self-protective person; if it's on the DC side we may meet people with caution, and could appear guarded, not easy to get to know.

"Why would it be helpful to work on the Ego planets? What will it offer me?"

In order to live our lives with greater self-knowledge and understanding, and ultimately get more out of life, we need to know as much about ourselves as we can. Many people say that they think they know themselves pretty well already, and maybe they do. But if you are choosing to work toward greater self-knowledge using astrological psychology, then it would be a huge omission not to explore the possibilities and solutions to any problems which your own natal chart can reveal. This is especially so with the ego planets. By understanding which of these we relate to most strongly, identify with most closely and live through, we can then begin to integrate, combine and unify their energies in our daily lives. The maxim here is *"Live the strongest ego planet and the weaker ones will integrate themselves."*

The API (UK) Diploma Course in Astrological Psychology gives guidelines on how to ascertain which of the three ego planets is the strongest, but this is something that is not always easy to judge. It takes an ongoing working experience of many charts and individuals, built up over a period of time, to be able to do this with some confidence, as well as a grounded and honest understanding of ourselves and how our own ego planets function. The practical work in this chapter is aimed at advancing this understanding.

Sun and the Mind ☉

Most people are familiar with their "Sun Sign" qualities and characteristics. But the Sun itself, as the star at the centre of our solar system, represents in the chart our autonomous self-awareness. The Sun has a cardinal quality, giving it the drive to be assertive, go-ahead and initiatory. The Hubers refer to the Sun as the part of the ego which allows us to reflect upon ourselves, to know ourselves and deliberately change things (see *The Planets and their Psychological Meaning*, page 32.) The Sun is the sense of self we have through our ability to make decisions and use the mind. It's our capacity to choose, making conscious choices and taking responsibility for ourselves.

The Sun can be likened to a film director, the conductor of an orchestra, the head of a large company or the leader of an expedition – as such it represents how we direct and use our will based on decisions we've made. It leads the way, and the rest of the planets, our psychological drives, follow. The Sun signifies our individuality, that part of us which can truly shine and makes us stand out from the crowd. It's our strength and power, our personal sense of "I". It's also our ability to discriminate and judge clearly, to think and to be creative.

Exercise – Sun/Mind (1)

Without stopping to think too much about what you write (and you could draw some things too if you find this easier), jot down what the Sun means for you. To help you focus on this exercise, you could draw on your experience of

- Phrases, actions, movements and sounds you associate with the Sun

- Music, animals, colours, creatures that remind you of the Sun

- Any manifestations of the solar principle in your everyday environment

For example, you might want to include "cat" under animals because cats are very solar creatures. Not only do they love the warmth of the Sun, they are strongly independent and don't have a marked need for people, as dogs (who are lunar) do.

Our mindset and the way we go about making decisions and using the will is going to be coloured by which sign the Sun is in, and which of the four elements is involved. A fiery Sun will express itself in a more volatile way than a practical earthy Sun; a watery Sun will be more emotionally attuned than an airy Sun which seeks ideas and likes to communicate.

There follows a further exercise to help you start thinking about your Sun.

Exercise – Sun/Mind (2)

Write down in your own words descriptions of your Sun:
- In the sign it's in
- In the element it's in (Fire, Earth, Air Water)

Base this on **your own real life experience** and on what you know about yourself – remember that no-one knows more about this particular topic than you do!

Some other suggestions for connecting with the energy of your Sun and exploring it further would be for you to:

- Start a collection of pictures which express the quality of the Sun for you. These could be pictures that you see in magazines, or they could be photographs, post cards, art cards or even drawings or paintings you've done yourself.

- Make a collage or picture to express in a creative and non-verbal way how your own Sun shines. You'll need to set aside time for this, together with a selection of magazines, tissue paper, coloured paper, gummed shapes, coloured foils, felt, wool, textured paper, crayons etc. plus scissors and glue. If you decide to undertake this project, you will be calling upon the imaginative qualities of your Moon as well as the creativity of your Sun – and your end product will satisfy Saturn's ability to manifest something in physical form.

Finally, here are some Sun/mind questions to help you focus more on the mind/will nature of the Sun. Make some brief notes for yourself as you respond to these questions.

1. Do I have my own goals?
2. Can I make a decision and see it through?
3. Do I know where I'm going and what I want to do?
4. Do I have a sense of purpose?
5. Am I taking enough opportunities to steer my life?

Moon and the Feelings ☽

The Moon, according to the Hubers, symbolises our feeling self (see *The Planets and their Psychological Meaning*, page 37) and our drive to make contact with others, and it gives us sensitivity and self-awareness through the emotions. The Moon has a Mutable quality, making it flexible, adaptable, reflective, mobile and fluid. It is associated with our capacity to give and receive love, something that is important to us as children and remains so throughout life. It acts as a mirror because we use the Moon to reflect what we receive from others, and this can influence how we react to them as we sense and respond emotionally. The Moon also represents our inner child, so it can be our spontaneity, our ability to have fun, to play, to interact, feel sad, angry, smile, laugh and so on.

Feelings can pervade our lives and unfortunately we're not always aware of how they are able to take over and dominate. If we're feeling sad and miserable, ill-at-ease or unwell, or are bursting with joy and happiness, these emotions are going to show up very clearly in the way we look, move and behave. Of course, we may have received messages, conditioning and expectations during childhood which have discouraged us from revealing feelings of anger, sadness, elation or excitement to the world at large. If this is the case, then we will probably repress our feelings and hold them tightly inside, fearing their non-acceptance by others. Unexpressed feelings don't go away, they stay within us and are held by the body. Negative emotions which are not expressed can fester away and cause physical discomfort such as tension headaches and digestive upsets. They can contribute to the onset of illness. Positive emotions such as enthusiasm, love and joy will want to burst out but may be waiting for permission to do so. In most cases, we can give ourselves permission to express feelings that are held inside, even if we only express them in private and for ourselves to begin with. If we find that the blocks that prevent us from expressing our feelings are too big to overcome alone, then the help of a counsellor or therapist would be an option to consider.

> ### Exercise – Moon/Feelings (1)
>
> In order to get you thinking about your Moon, the following short exercise aims to help you connect with the Moon through something from your childhood. You may want to close your eyes to do this exercise after first reading it through:
>
> - Reflect for a few minutes on an episode, event or situation you experienced in your childhood. You may find it helps to bring to mind a photograph of yourself in a particular place or situation. Perhaps you'll remember where you were, or what you were wearing. Don't censor or judge the episode that comes to mind – it may be happy, sad, scary, amusing, exciting… just allow it to be with you now. Allow yourself to be taken back there in your imagination and really try to get the feel of the situation. Allow any feelings you had about that episode in your life to come back to you as well. See if you can connect what this experience from childhood has awakened and recall what you did at the time to express your feelings of excitement or sadness or whatever emotion was evoked in you.
>
> Then slowly open your eyes and return to the place you're in now, and make a few notes for yourself on this experience of connecting with your inner child and Moon.

Exercise – Moon/Feelings (2)

The energies and qualities of the Moon can be awakened in many different ways, and you might like to try these short exercises. You'll need pen and paper for this.

- Jot down 4-6 things which make you **feel good**, concentrating on the physical and emotional. For example, it might make you feel good to go for a run, workout at the gym, meet an old friend, enjoy food, receive warmth, love, acceptance. Concentrate on those things which nourish and nurture your inner child.

- Write down 6 things which are **fun** for you. For example, these may include cooking, buying or making clothes, listening to or making music, going to films and shows, dancing, playing games, going on holiday or out for the day. Concentrate on those things which nourish and nurture the playful part of your inner child.

- Note down any **fantasies** that you have – allow your imagination to flow. For example, you may connect with your daydreams, fantasy characters you would like to be and places you would like to visit. Give your imagination full rein so you can nourish and nurture the magical part of your inner child.

- Jot down 3-4 ways (or more) in which you express your **creativity**. Make a note of anything that blocks or stops this creativity being expressed – might this be linked to the aspects the Moon has in your chart? For example, Saturn could give the creative expression of the Moon a tough time, but it could also be very useful in helping to harness, structure and consolidate the creativity.

> ### Exercise – Moon/Feelings (3)
>
> Finally, here are some questions which will help you focus on the feelings aspect of the Moon. Make some brief notes for yourself as you respond to these questions.
>
> 1. How big a part do my feelings play in my everyday life?
> 2. Am I making enough contacts with people?
> 3. Am I able to state my emotional needs or feelings?
> 4. Am I able to ask for what I want or need?

The Moon and the multitude of feelings and emotions it symbolises is often a neglected area of life. Working with this planet can be a key to unlocking the frequently found theme of relationships which often shows up in charts, since feelings and emotional responses are closely bound up with this area of life. My own experience of working with clients, along with their charts and life experience, is that many of them are seeking to unblock and free up their feelings in order to live happier and more fulfilled lives. This, in turn, is likely to have a positive effect on health because if feelings can be expressed, they are not held tightly in place within the body where they can cause dis-ease and ill health.

Saturn and the Body ♄

You will probably already have a few ideas of your own about the symbolic meaning of Saturn in the natal chart, and which psychological drives this planet might represent. Saturn has a fixed quality, making it concerned with structure, form, consolidation and stability. If we take a very broad view of which objects and experiences in the wider world around us could come under the general heading of "Saturn", we might come up with rocks, mountains, bodies, organisations, solid structures or buildings made of stone, institutions, boundaries, rules, restraints, practicality, habits, a wise teacher, car seat belts, a child's safety harness, time, shoulds and oughts, interconnecting physical systems within the body, material goods, holding back, scaffolding, skeletons… and many, many more. You may well have additional ideas and associations of your own, and you are encouraged to participate in the practical activities which follow.

Bruno and Louise Huber speak of Saturn as the physical self (see *The Planets and their Psychological Meaning*, page 41), representing the physical manifestation of ourselves through our bodies. Saturn can be experienced through the way we express ourselves and take care of ourselves physically.

Exercise – Saturn/Body (1)

Take a few moments now to jot down as many words, phrases or associations as you can as to what Saturn means for you. It is worth taking the time to do this as it will help you to build up your own references and key words for this planet. Your list should be organic and continue to grow because you can return to it whenever you get a new association or idea.

Exercise – Saturn/Body (2)

Stop for a moment and think of all the ways in which you can express yourself through your body. This may cover all manner of things from what you eat, to how often you bath or shower, to taking physical exercise to what you wear, and how you present yourself to the world. Make some brief notes for yourself about this.

- As you read these words, become aware of your body. You may be sitting in a chair, lying down, or even standing up. Is your body comfortable or does it need to move slightly to adjust its position? If so, let it do this. Be aware of which parts of your body are touching the chair, the floor or wherever you are as you read this, and really allow yourself to feel your body physically in the position and posture it is in.

- Now shift your attention and awareness to how your body feels in terms of temperature – is it hot and sticky, cold, cool, or comfortable and just right? How do the clothes you are wearing feel? Are they tight in places? Would you like to loosen your waistband, take off your sweater, undo a top button, kick off your shoes? Does your body feel restricted in any way by what you're wearing, or have you got it right today and feel comfortable?

- Turn your attention to the inside of your body. How are the various interconnected physical systems it is composed of getting on today? Is your digestive system letting you know that you shouldn't have had that extra helping, or it is telling you that you're empty and peckish and looking forward to your next meal? Is your excretory system letting you know that you'll need to visit the loo soon? Or maybe you can feel your heart beating, or a pulse somewhere throbbing, so you are aware of your circulatory system.

> ### Exercise – Saturn/Body (3)
>
> Finally, here are some questions to help you focus more on the physical aspect of Saturn. Make some brief notes for yourself as you respond to these questions.
>
> 1. Am I giving my own physical self enough care and attention?
> 2. How am I looking after my own body, my own structure?
> 3. Am I aware of the needs of my body?
> 4. Am I aware of the capabilities of my body?

The qualities of restraint, restriction and the need for security, which are all associated with Saturn, can be experienced on the emotional level when the feelings are engaged and we have doubts and fears. Because of this, we often limit and even sabotage ourselves in various ways. We doubt our own abilities. We keep our feelings under wraps and hold back their true expression because we feel guilty, afraid or even tongue-tied if we have never been encouraged to express ourselves in this way for fear of upsetting people, or breaking social rules and expectations. Maybe we are afraid of gaining the disapproval of someone in a position of authority.

If you let Saturn hold you back in any way where **you** are not willing and in agreement for this holding back to take place, you will buying in to allowing Saturn to be like a heavy millstone that will hold you down. We all need some boundaries, structures, guidelines and safety nets in life, and if we can live in harmony with these then Saturn will become more like a wise and caring mentor who guides, but does not hold us back.

Exercise – Saturn/Body (4)

- Stop for a moment now and check whether you have any doubts and fears, or if there are any areas in your life where you might hold back and not say truly what is going on for you for fear of being judged and being made to feel guilty for what you are doing. Explore your emotional defences – what are they? How do you put up a "drawbridge" and defend yourself from either getting hurt or from getting close and being more open? Sometimes, of course, it is more appropriate to use our defence mechanisms in order to stay safe… yet we need to use these consciously, so that they do not use us. And if we are using them consciously we will also know when it is appropriate to bring them into play, and when it is not, thus integrating Saturn and the Moon.

- Take a few moments to recall those situations and things in your life right now (you could also draw on situations from the past) where you hold, or held back. Allow yourself to connect with some of these issues, without judgement, and make a few notes for yourself. If you can, note in which instances you were aware of your own fears, or psychological restraints, your need not to rock the boat and so on.

Astrologically, Saturn has a rather negative reputation. I remember it was described to me as "The Grim Reaper" when I was starting to learn astrology – hardly a tempting planet to get to know better! Yet without Saturnian qualities life would be a disorganised mess. I have given a lot of study and thought to this planet and to how its more pessimistic attributes can be viewed in a different light and used positively. But that demands conscious awareness on our part.

Exercise – Saturn/Body (5)

Think of ways in which you might use Saturn in a positive, discriminating way that helps you to move through life smoothly, efficiently and with good organisation. For example, you might decide to learn something, perhaps a new skill or a topic that is new to you. The learning you undertake will require dedication and application to master the subject matter, and it is here that Saturn can help and support you working at the level of the mind. Saturn-type learning does not take place quickly – it takes time, it's like a long-term project where the learning takes root, nestles down somewhere in your unconscious or subconscious and slowly grows, flowers and comes to fruition.

- Take some time now to ponder on how Saturn energies work for you at the level of the mind and how they can be integrated with your Sun. How organised are you? Do you have a broad structure to your days? Do you operate within a framework which includes both yourself and others? Are you aware of your responsibilities without letting them tie you – or do you feel shackled by them? Be aware that **you** have made these decisions in your life to let them either feel comfortable, or bog you down.

- How do you organise your life? Do you make lists that you are dependent upon, or are you able to use memory to help you connect with those things needing attention? When you learn something, does the learning go in deep – does this happen just sometimes, or every time? Have you ever met someone who was very wise, maybe older than yourself (but not necessarily so) who acted as your mentor or guide as you learned something new? Maybe it was something about yourself that you learned, and you will always regard this person as someone special who helped you to connect with the benevolent, teaching/learning aspect of Saturn within.

Make notes in response to these questions. You will be able to refer to them in the section which follows.

Practical Work with Sun, Moon and Saturn in the Chart

There are several points to take into consideration when assessing the comparative strength or weakness of the ego planets, and these will be set out as suggestions to use alongside your chart. Most of these points are explained in *The Cosmic Egg Timer* and they are covered in depth in the API (UK) Diploma Course. Some of them have already been discussed in Chapter 1 and you are encouraged to incorporate what you've learned from the practical exercises there into this exploration. You'll need to have your chart handy to refer to.

"What kind of things should I look for?"

A brief list would include the following, which are further amplified in the subsequent sections and exercises:

Where are the ego planets positioned in the chart?
What colour aspects does each receive?
What aspect pattern is each one a part of?
Which houses are they in?
Are they strong, average or weak by position in sign and house?
Are any of them on the Low Point of a house?
Are they unaspected or intercepted?

Position of Ego Planets in the Chart

- **Saturn**, because it is associated with form, manifestation, stability and security needs is best positioned in the lower hemisphere of the chart.
- **Moon**, because it is associated with contact and connects on an emotional, feeling level, is best positioned across the I/You axis of the chart.
- **Sun**, because it is associated with sense of self as an autonomous individual, is best positioned in the upper hemisphere of the chart.

The following chart shows the ego planets in these positions.

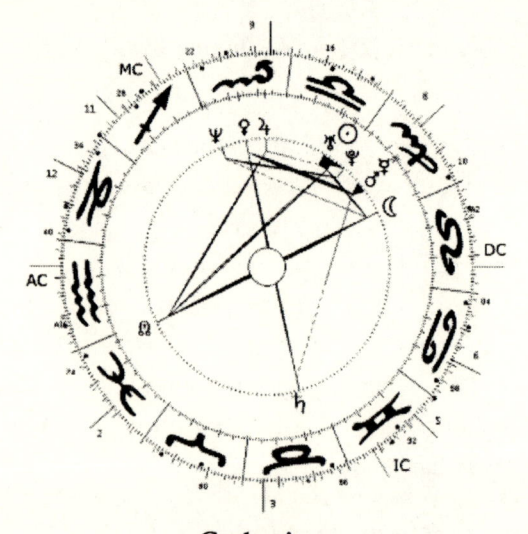

Catherine
27.09.1970, 17:10, Manchester, UK

Aspects to the Ego Planets

The colours of the aspects each convey a different quality of energy which will "light up" your ego planets and motivate them to act in a certain way. You will recall from Chapter 1 that red aspects bring cardinal, active "doing" energy to the planets they connect with, green aspects give mutable, sensitive, seeking energy, and blue aspects give fixed energy which is concerned with stability, security and simply "being".

Exercise – Aspect Colours to Ego Planets

Check out the colours of aspects to your Sun, Moon and Saturn. What is the **balance** of colours in the aspects each of your ego planets has? Very red or not red at all? More green than anything else? Or overwhelmingly blue? Maybe one or more of your ego planets is in a conjunction? If so, you'll need to consider the close binding quality of the conjunction aspect with the planet or planets involved, along with the potential for new qualities to emerge from within your personality from this combination of planets.

> ### Exercise – Ego Planets in Aspect Patterns
>
> Which aspect pattern or patterns are your ego planets involved in? One or several? What are the patterns and what information do they offer you regarding the ego planets they include? Are you aware of how your ego planets operate within these patterns? What is the shaping and motivation of the aspect pattern? Does the Sun command and lead the way, Moon enable you to express your feelings via this pattern, or Saturn to manifest something tangible in the world?
>
> Which planets do your Sun, Moon and Saturn connect with through the overall aspect structure? How might the connection with these planets help or hinder their expression? Do any of your ego planets connect with one of the transpersonal planets – Uranus, Neptune and Pluto – and if so, how does this affect their expression?

"What if all three ego planets are in the same aspect pattern?"

Bruno Huber has suggested that if all three ego planets are connected in this way, there could be an already-existing sense of ego integration which might inhibit further growth. As part of our process of development is to achieve an integration of the personality, including being able to experience the world through a balance of body, feelings and mind, then having all three ego planets in the same aspect pattern could limit or stifle this process. Childhood conditioning and the need to survive will often create an imbalance in the way we approach the world through the ego, so we may grow into adulthood more identified with just the body, just the feelings or just the mind. In such a case, we will meet the world and interact with it predominantly through this one aspect of the ego. Therefore, part of the process of psychological development is to discover and bring into consciousness whichever aspect of the ego was repressed or not encouraged to develop fully in childhood.

Ego Planet Positioning

It is suggested that you explore the positioning of the ego planets in your chart by working through the following exercise.

> ### Exercise – Ego Planet Positioning
>
> Consider each of your ego planets in the context of the house it is in because this will tell you how it is placed in relation to the rest of the world. Be honest with yourself about this as it will show you in which area of life each ego planet makes contact with the environment, and where it seeks expression and recognition.
>
> ### Strength by Sign
>
> If your Sun, Moon or Saturn are positioned between 8° and 18° of the **sign** they are in, this will make them strong by sign. If they are placed at 11½°, they are in the strongest position by sign that they can be; the weakest places for a planet to be are at the beginning and end of a sign.
>
> ### Strength by House
>
> Now look at where your Sun, Moon and Saturn are positioned in the **house** they are in. Do you have one or more of them placed just before a house cusp, where they will feel stressed and under pressure to "perform"? Are they right on the cusp of a house, which will ensure that their energies and abilities are readily noticed by the surrounding environment? Maybe they are placed on or near the Balance Point where they can work effectively and efficiently without depleting their energy and running out of steam?
>
> ### Low Point Positioning
>
> Do you have one or more ego planet(s) positioned on or near the **Low Point** of a house? If so, it could be difficult to satisfactorily express the energy of such a planet. If your Sun is on a Low Point, it may feel as if no-one notices you or gives due recognition to your individuality and authority.

[Exercise continues on next page.]

A Low Point Moon could suggest you spend more time connecting with and mulling over your feelings and emotional needs, but when you come to ask for these to be met, the world is simply not interested. With a Low Point Saturn you might think you are well-organised and law-abiding, and will expect people to recognise this. You will feel misunderstood when the world sees you as disorganised and lacking in self-discipline. With a Low Point ego planet you will go out of your way to gain recognition for the attributes you are sure you have. But the more noise and fuss you make about this, the more irritated the environment becomes, and quickly loses interest in what you have to offer.

Conflict between Sign and House Position
An ego planet which is strong by sign, but placed on the Low Point of the house is likely to produce a heightened sense of frustration when the energy of this planet is expressed. Despite its strength by sign, it will come out "muffled" by its house position when shown to the environment. Conversely, an ego planet which is weak by sign, but placed prominently just before or even on a house cusp, will feel overwhelming demands to "get it right" out in world, and will struggle to maintain its momentum and stay the course.

If any of the above factors has particular relevance to an ego planet in your chart, make some notes now on your related experiences of this planet. Is there anything you might choose to do to change your responses and behaviour?

ᄆ ᄆ ᄆ ᄆ ᄆ

Although we have been looking specifically at the strength of the ego planets by sign and by house, the same principles apply to all the planets. The strength of a planet by both sign and house should always be considered as should any conflict between these positions, as described above. Some examples are given in the following chapter.

Unaspected Ego Planets

Without aspects, a planet is not going to be integrated into the chart and the psyche as a whole. This is especially so with an unaspected ego planet. Unaspected planets look to the environment to shape their experiences and subsequent responses. With an unaspected Sun you might rely heavily on outside influences to give you a sense of who you are and how to think; unaspected Moon will soak up feelings from whoever they come into contact with and unaspected Saturn could have a haphazard sense of organisation and depend on others coming to their rescue. Any such deficits and challenges can be worked with consciously, but the person themselves has to be willing to cooperate in this process.

Intercepted Ego Planets

As with the Low Point, intercepted ego planets can also be a source of frustration. Being intercepted in a sign with no house cusps means that the planet has no direct route for expressing itself in the environment. It has to draw upon the energies of other planets connected to it by aspects, in order to channel its own energy out into the surrounding environment.

Example – Strongest Ego Planet

We will now put some of these factors together in considering the case of Dan (chart on next page) at a workshop on the ego planets. Dan initially felt that his Sun was the strongest ego planet and spoke of his strong Sagittarian nature and his own sense of self-confidence. Note that he has unaspected Jupiter in the 5th house, emphasising a Sagittarian/Jupiterian enthusiasm for life. Dan talked about his experience of his ego planets at the workshop, responding to the questions on Sun, Moon and Saturn set out earlier in this chapter. He offered his chart for discussion by the group, who collectively assessed Saturn as being his strongest ego planet. Dan was somewhat surprised to see his Sun was regarded as being comparatively weak when set alongside Saturn.

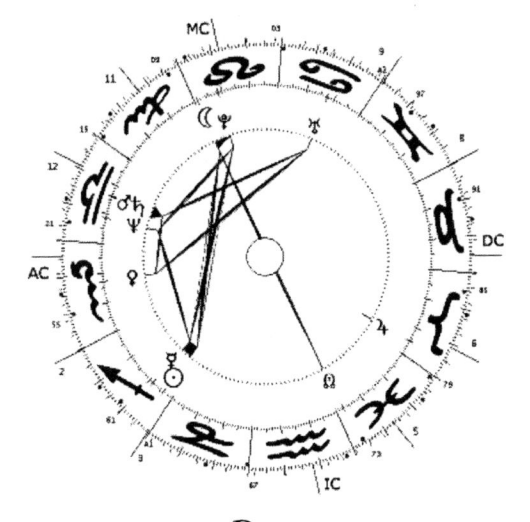

Dan
19.12.1951, 03:45, Chester, UK

Dan's Sun is in a stressed position by house as it is in the stress area approaching the 3rd cusp. Moon is in the fixed zone of the 10th house, between the Balance and Low Points, and Saturn is placed just after the cusp of the 12th house. This is a "quiet" house by nature but because Saturn comes just after the cusp it is strongly placed within it.

By sign, Dan's Sun is at 26° making it rather weak; Moon is at 29° – even weaker and almost at the end of Leo. Saturn is at 13° making it the strongest of the three ego planets by sign.

Assessing the strength of the positions of Sun, Moon and Saturn in the chart was less easy. The Sun, which would be most comfortable in the upper hemisphere of the chart, is the lowest of the three ego planets. Saturn, which would be most comfortable below the horizon, is above it, albeit tucked away in the 12th house and not far from the horizon. The Moon, however, is "on show" and is the highest of the ego planets. Although the Moon is optimally placed when on the I/You Encounter axis of the chart, it was agreed by group participants that as it is the ego planet most concerned with contact, feelings and emotional needs, it was likely to be the strongest by position as it is well-placed for "recognition" up in the 10th house. In addition to this, it is empowered and intensified by its conjunction to Pluto and although very weak by sign, it is still a Leo Moon! Dan's behaviour when he arrived slightly late at the workshop bears this out; amidst good humoured joking about where he would sit (he chose to sit on a couch between two women) he was easily able to focus the awareness of the group on himself and receive their full attention.

Assessing the significance of the aspects to his ego planets was also difficult. The Moon was assessed as strongest as it presented more opportunities to connect with the rest of the chart than did the Sun or Saturn. Saturn has one red and one green aspect; Moon has two blue and one red; Sun has only blue, although both Sun and Moon are conjunct another planet.

Dan spoke of feeling as though he was "in a trench", having always been aware of his Sagittarian Sun and Leo Moon. The 2nd house Sun for him represents his property investment business – a source of financial security. He is also well-travelled, and was formerly a DJ, living out and expressing his Leo Moon high in the chart. He said he feels caught in the blue trines between Sun and Moon, as though he has to go back and forth between these two aspects himself. He had come to the workshop looking for a way out of this.

He said he couldn't relate to Saturn being assessed as his strongest ego planet. Dan is fit, healthy and in good shape physically. He dresses casually but with an air of smartness and attention to appearance. This was pointed out to him, and he was asked how much attention he paid to his own physical well-being. He said that he worked out regularly and strenuously – running, playing sport, mountain biking etc. If he missed his workouts for a couple of days he felt bad, and this included feeling bad about himself and less confident. It was suggested to him that this was a reflection of his strong Saturn helping him develop and work on his comparatively weaker Sun through what he gained from his physical workouts. He talked of how he works out early in the morning before it's light, going running and swimming. He admitted that this is challenging, sometimes punishing, and that he is challenging himself physically and competing with himself.

There seems to be a strong element of training the Sun and the will at work here, of somehow unconsciously working towards integrating the ego planets, particularly the Sun. Dan said that this had given him a lot to think about and focus upon in terms of himself and how he operates, and offered the following feedback approximately three weeks after the workshop:

> *"I see myself as very typically Sagittarian and with an enthusiasm for travel, ideas, philosophy and so on. My 2nd house Sun represents survival for me, through my property investment business. It is also in the 1st quadrant of the chart, the one associated with survival. I seem to really wake up inside under difficult situations, especially when training, i.e. windsurfing in rain, skiing in blizzards, mountain biking in the foulest, wettest, muddiest conditions.*
>
> *The Leo Moon you may judge for yourself! Your earlier observations made me cringe at my own behaviour, but I CAN'T HELP IT!!*
>
> *Saturn – I never realised the connection, but yes, I want order in my life and self-discipline on a physical level. I have achieved constant discipline physically (and get ill when I don't) yet organisationally I have periods of setting myself "straight" and focus on paperwork etc., and then fall back into chaos. I hate the chaos and want to be organised but can't maintain it. I see the fact that Sun and Saturn are in separate aspect patterns as indicating this struggle and lack of integration."*

Chapter 4

Integrating with the Environment

How we meet and interact with the environment around us is an important feature of the Huber Method. The astrological houses, which represent the environment, the outside world and arenas of life experience and expression, are given prominence. Information obtained using the Hubers' Dynamic House System can indicate how easily we might integrate with the world around us, as well as show where we might run into problems and find it more difficult to express ourselves successfully in certain areas of life.

In this chapter we look in depth at the houses, together with other aspects of the Huber Method which offer insights into how we fit into our environment. First, we explore our primary environment – the family – and the effect that childhood influences might have had on us in our early years. These influences may still affect our lives now resulting in behaviour and drives, which might otherwise be helpful and useful to us, being blocked or suppressed. The ways in which we were brought up and conditioned by our parents or those who raised us in our formative years can remain with us well into adult years, and there is no denying that parental influences play a vital role in the way we interact with the world around us.

The Family Model

When working with the Family Model, a technique which is unique to the Huber Method, it is important to bear in mind that our view of our parents and the way we were raised is going to be subjective. Drawing on childhood memories and impressions can be painful; if these are not so pleasant it is probable that we will have screened out certain memories and experiences. Because of this, it is essential that we recognise and respect any feelings and recollections that arise, both for ourselves and for others if we are working on the chart of a friend or family member. Exploring the Family Model can be a sensitive matter, and should be approached with this in mind.

Before looking further at the Family Model, it is suggested that you do the practical exercise opposite, to get you thinking about yourself and your parents as you were growing up. You may want to refer back to what you've noted down as you work through the next section.

Family Model – Theory

"Which planets are involved in the Family Model?"

The three ego planets come into play again here, but this time they represent one of the mother/father/child roles.

- The **Sun** represents the role of father ☉
- The **Moon** represents that of the child ☽
- **Saturn** represents the role of mother ♄

"Saturn doesn't make me think of mother! How does this work?"

Remember that Saturn represents the **role** of mother – not your mother herself. The qualities associated with this planet include laws and rules, guidelines, structures, boundaries and frameworks. Laws govern behaviour. If the law says we have to behave in a certain way in order to fit into society and be

Exercise – Childhood Memories

Draw a large circle on a sheet of paper and divide it into 3 segments, naming them "Mother", "Father" and "Child".

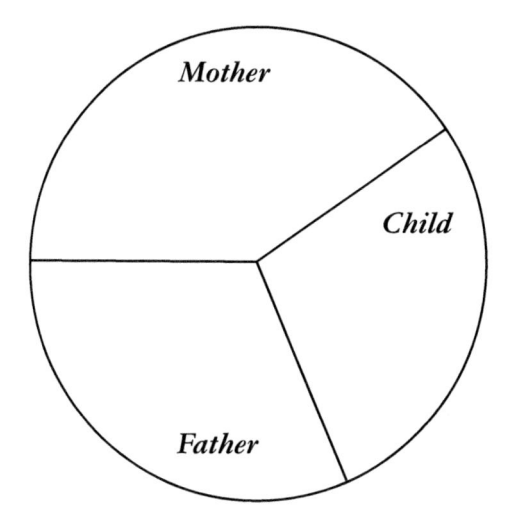

Brainstorm and write down as many memories and associations as you can for each one in turn in the appropriate segment. For example, you could note down the kind of people your mother and father were, and what you were like as a child. Use your memory associations of the tastes, smells, habits, talents, abilities that were evident in your family, together with the interests your parents had. Note down any phrases that were used, clothes worn, music played or heard, places remembered and visited, and so on. Allow yourself to conjure up a full sensory memory of yourself as a child, and of your mother and father or the people who brought you up and acted in these roles. Go back as far as you can… let the memories flow… and note down what stands out for you and what is important for you. You will probably find that you want to return from time to time to add extra things as the memories bubble up, so allow yourself plenty of time to do this exercise.

accepted by it, then we will modify our behaviour to conform with this. If we do not obey the laws and rules by which society operates we are subject to punishment, and depending on what it is we have done we may feel guilty about our behaviour too. If, in the eyes of our mother, we have done something wrong as a child we can easily feel desolated and fearful that she will withdraw her love, caring and attention from us. Mothers tell us what we should and should not do. If we go beyond these set boundaries and are found out, it is highly likely that we will end up feeling guilty.

Saturn, as you read earlier, is also associated with the body and involvement in the physical, material aspect of life. We experience this as babies and children, through our mother's touch, as the mother/baby relationship is especially tactile. Mothers provide physical care, and cater for physical and survival needs as we grow up. They wash, dress and feed us. They guide and teach us, giving reminders about cleaning teeth, washing hands, and tidying toys away. Saturn, in the role of mother, generally has our well-being at heart (even if it didn't always feel like it at the time), but we can also be physically and emotionally inhibited and restrained by the Saturnian rules imposed by her. Saturn as mother in protective mode is the one who tells us not to do things for the sake of our safety. For example, you could have been told "Don't walk on that wall – you might fall off" just as you'd started to master the skill of balancing along the top of the wall and were feeling pretty good about it! The chances are that you still walked along the tops of walls when your mother wasn't with you, experiencing these feelings of daring and accomplishment mixed with slight guilt and apprehension because you were told not to do it, you might have fallen off, and you could have been found out.

"OK, how does the Sun fit into the role of father?"
The Sun represents the father as he is generally the family member who goes out into the world and has, from the child's point of view, adventures and a wider experience of life

outside the home as opposed to the mother, who stays at home providing nurturing, protection and all those do's and don'ts. At this point, we have to acknowledge that what is described here is a conventional set-up and that family roles are in the process of change. The person providing the mothering may not be the natural mother, who may go out to work. Nowadays some aspects of the Saturn role fall to other family members or professional child care institutions. It may be the father who stays at home whilst the mother is the main bread winner. If this is the case, the father will assume both roles for some of the time. Likewise if the mother is a single parent she will fulfil both Sun and Saturn roles.

However, as we still live in a patriarchal society, and for the purposes of fully illustrating the Family Model, the role of father is to set an example of leadership for the child, to be head of the household, make major decisions, go out to work, provide for the family, in command and in a position of authority. He is the parent who actively **encourages** the child to walk on the top of the wall, saying "You can do it!" The Sun is associated with the mind, with decision-making processes and innate creativity. The Sun, in the role of father, supports the child in learning how to make up his or her mind, think for himself and be self-assertive. This may lead to conflict with the Saturn/mother role as the child will eventually reach a stage of development when it thinks it knows best and will openly defy and challenge the rules and limitations imposed by the mother. The child will then assert its own individuality and sense of "I am."

"How does the Moon fit into the Family Model?"

The Moon in this family triad represents the child who wants love, contact with others, and the fulfilment of its emotional needs. The feeling nature is involved, making the Moon significant as its functions stay alive, growing with us, and are present when we become adults. We each of us have a small but nonetheless very special child within who has basic needs which may go unheard, unexpressed and unmet. The child, represented by the Moon, is sensitive, impressionable and often very needy. In babyhood and childhood these needs for love, nourishment, warmth, safety, guidance and encouragement to express creativity will hopefully have been provided by the parents. A child wants to be hugged, loved and cared for. As children, we learn by example, and if we didn't receive the hugs and love we wanted from those who brought us up, we're not going to find it easy to express this part of our emotional selves as adults. Inner child needs such as these are present when we're grown up. If they were neglected, ignored or repressed by the environment we can, if we so choose, learn how to express them as adults, and we can become both mother and father to ourselves. Being grown-up is not needing our parents any more as parents, but fulfilling those roles for ourselves.

"How can we do this?"

- We can develop our own will, using the Sun, and consciously behave in a more autonomous manner. We can be aware of taking responsibility for ourselves and our various needs, honing our thinking and decision-making processes, remaining alert and self-aware, nurturing our creativity and seeking ways to express it. We can consciously choose to create, shape and mould our life in directions which are positive and rewarding.

- We can draw on the strength of Saturn by tapping into our ability to nurture ourselves and ensure our physical safety. We can make sure we eat properly and wisely for our health, take care of our bodies, and are able to fit into and contribute to the society we've been born into.

- The grown-up Moon has to stay alert to its emotional needs, finding ways of expressing these and having them met. The adult Moon can strengthen and express its child-like qualities such as sensitivity, spontaneity, the ability to enjoy sources of delight, the ability to play and the ability to make contact with others.

> **Exercise – Moon Child**
>
> Make a list of all the ways in which you can nurture, encourage or "parent" your own Moon for yourself. For example, you could **choose to give yourself** the love, praise, encouragement, positive feedback and rewards that you need.

"Does it matter where the Sun, Moon and Saturn are positioned in the chart?"

From the subjective child's-eye-view of the Family Model, the planet which was highest in the chart will have been the family member which dominated the domestic environment. Generally speaking, the higher the planet, the greater the significance and influence that family member will have had. The Sun/father figure is ideally placed at the top of the chart in a position of authority where he can be seen and acknowledged. The Moon/child is best placed on the AC/DC axis where making contact with others is easiest. Saturn/mother figure fares best in the lower hemisphere of the chart where Saturn's grounding qualities are most at home and can act as a foundation stone, giving solidity and support to the family from this position. Of course, things all too often do not conform to the "ideal" so here are a few points to bear in mind:

- Sun in the lower hemisphere may indicate a father who was a slight disappointment to the child; maybe he was not at home very much, or was not really "present" or engaged with the family scene when he was.

- Moon in the lower hemisphere, particularly in the 4th house, will suggest a child who is reluctant to leave the comfort and security of the home, or will feel smothered with love and unable to easily assert their own independence.

- Saturn in the upper hemisphere can indicate a mother who had her own career or who was not always there for the child, making him or her feel insecure and lacking in a firm base.

The way in which Sun, Moon and Saturn are grouped in relation to each other can be another indicator of how and where the child was encouraged to interact with the outside world. Are these planets close together, maybe in the same quadrant or close to each other in the same area of the chart? If so, this could indicate a close-knit family who did things together, or just kept themselves to themselves; it doesn't necessarily mean they all got on well together!

It is also worth checking the I/You sides of the chart if a grouping of Sun, Moon and Saturn is found here. Which side of the chart is the grouping on? Does the family group go out to meet the world and make contact on the "You" side, or is it more quietly positioned on the "I" side of the chart? Are Sun and Saturn on one side of the chart and Moon on the other, or are the three planets some distance apart, not connected and not close?

Examples – Family Model Grouping

If the grouping is at the top of the chart, this could indicate an outgoing family where the child tasted life outside of the family home and environment.

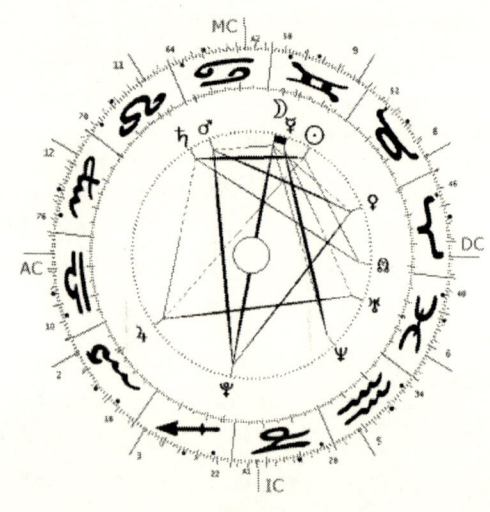

Jack
28.05.2006, 15:21 (14:21 GMT)
51.35 N, 03.00 W

4. Integrating with the Environment   81

If Sun, Moon and Saturn are grouped together at the bottom of the chart, it is possible that they did not stray far from their own locality.

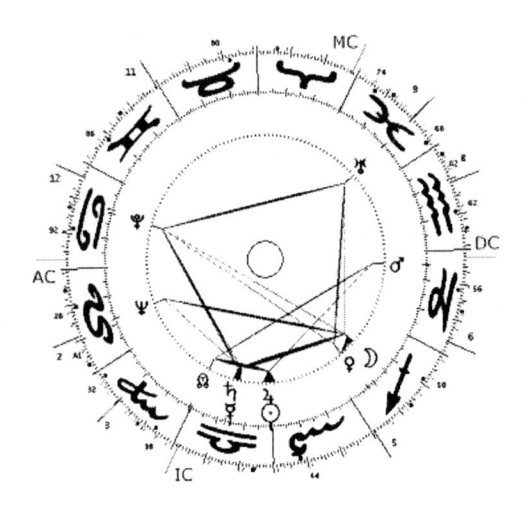

Phoebe
23.10.1922, 23:00 (22:00 GMT)
51.30 N, 00.10 W

The Moon involved in a conjunction with Sun and/or Saturn indicates that the child could grow up with difficulties in self-identification. It could take a lifetime's work to detach from the influence of the parent involved, and identification with this parent.

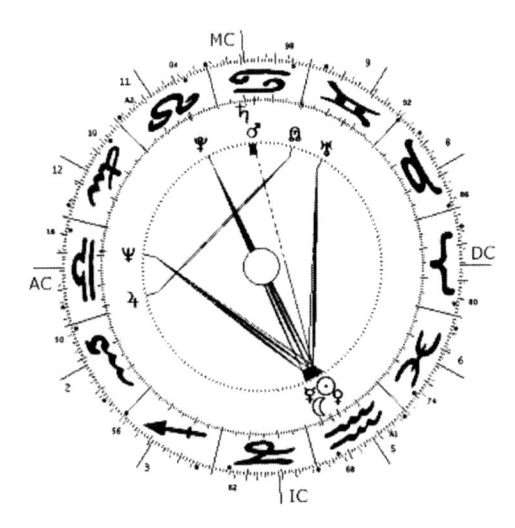

Claire
01.02.1946, 22:45 GMT
54.09 N, 02.02 W

Exercise – Family Model

Take a look at your own chart now and note which is the highest planet in your own Family Model, as well as observing any interesting features in the family grouping. Note also which houses the Sun, Moon and Saturn are in and see if this correlates with who was the most dominant member of this family triad. Identify the theme of the house involved for each planet. From this can you gain more information about the area of life that each family member was most comfortable in? Can you see how the family grouping could have affected the way you were encouraged or discouraged to integrate with the surrounding environment? Make notes for yourself about what you see in the Family Model in your own chart.

The Energy Balance – Planets in Houses

The houses in the chart represent the environment around us – our world – and it's worth considering first and foremost in this section exactly what is meant when we use the term "our world". What **is** your world? And where in the world are you? In order for you to explore this idea and give this section more focus, let's begin with a short practical exercise (opposite page).

Exercise – Your Houses

Think for a moment or two about your own world, the one that you inhabit which is unique to you. Using the diagram below as a guide, write down or do some sketch drawings of the different parts of your world that relate to each particular house or area of life experience. If you draw a larger copy of the diagram on a large sheet of paper, you will have plenty of space to complete the different sections.

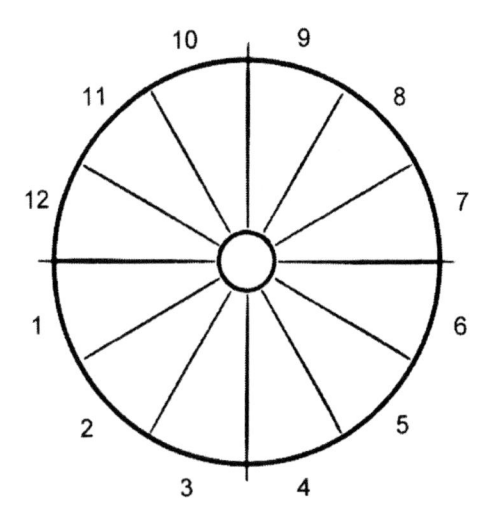

For example, in section 1 you might write or sketch your bedroom or your own space in your home; maybe your wardrobe or your desk would be there. Section 2 might be somewhere you feel safe and secure, or where you keep things you value. It could also be the place where you practise any particular talents and skills you have. Section 3 could be where you communicate with the outside world in a variety of ways – by email, phone, face to face etc. or where you go to find the information you need. When you have completed your diagram keep it to refer to later on, as it will provide a focus for when you come to consider the planets and their positions in the houses in your chart.

The houses relate to our spatial, physical environment. Right now I am writing this in my home, which is also sometimes used as venue for astrological psychology workshops. As "home" it is 4th house, but when used for workshops, for learning and sharing knowledge, it includes and incorporates 3rd/9th house activities. And when this happens, it also becomes a place for groups of like-minded people to meet and discuss ideas – a very 11th house activity. My home is also my place of work, which relates to the 6th house. From this, it's clear to see that the houses can spatially be much more than just one thing. Their boundaries overlap and are blurred, and it is we who define them. They can flow into each other and change and alter, depending on different needs and tasks in our lives, so we need to be aware when we, or someone else, has crossed the border between one spatial house area and another. This can happen when we bring work home from the office, or are rung up from work during holiday times or when we have a day's leave.

"What are the houses psychologically?"

If we explore the psychological meaning of the houses, we can form a more rounded and satisfying view of what they mean for us in real life terms. We will find many points of agreement with others as to the general meaning of each house as there are common themes for them all, but our own experience will differ from someone else's because each one of us is unique, as is our chart.

Exercise – Selected House

Choose one house from your chart which is empty, and one which has one or more planets in it, then spend a few minutes writing something about each of these houses. Describe each in terms of how you feel you operate within this house/area of life:

- What do you do there? What are your activities?
- How effective are you in there?
- How easily or comfortably do you feel drawn, or not drawn, to this area of life?
- Are there any particular difficulties associated with this area of life for you?
- What works smoothly and easily here?
- How do you feel when you are aware that you are there – "on stage" so to speak?
- What kind of response/reaction do you get from the environment when you are in that part of your world?

When you have completed these notes, take a look at your chart alongside what you have written and view your responses within the context of your chart as a whole. Note the interplay between the colours of the aspects to the planets in your chosen tenanted house, the aspect patterns that are involved, and how the hemispheres and quadrants of the chart relate to the houses you have chosen to look at. Record any observations that seem significant.

The Dynamic Energy Curve

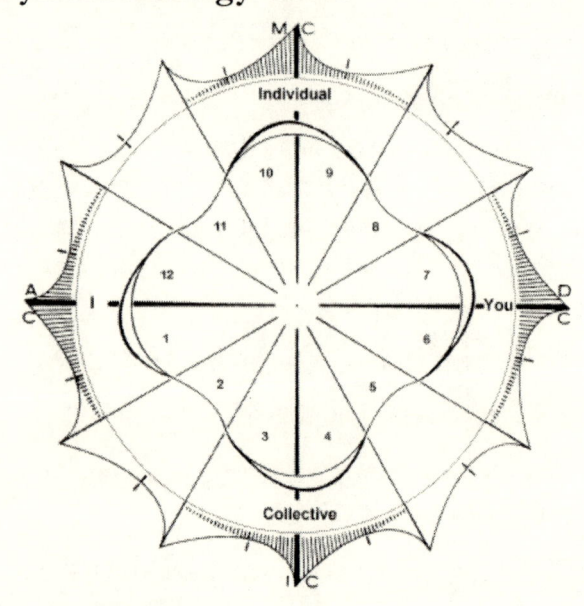

The energy curve diagram (introduced in *The Cosmic Egg Timer*) shows a wave-like curve of the peaks and troughs of available energy at any given place in the house system. The source of this energy comes from the centre of the chart and the diagram shows how it seeks to flow out into the world (the houses) via the aspects, the planets and the signs in which they are placed. Depending on where our planets are placed in this curve – on the crest or in the trough of the wave – this will relate to how we feel, respond and behave out in the world. Planets near the cusp of each house, where the wave peaks, will be more able to express themselves out in the world. Those on or near the Low Point – the trough of the wave – are likely to experience more difficulty in making themselves heard and recognised by the environment.

It will be useful at this stage to briefly recap the significant areas within the Dynamic Energy Curve. The psychological starting point of each house is the Low Point of the previous house. The **stress area** lies just before the cusp of the house. Planets placed here will be under stress to perform and respond to the demands and expectations of the environment, so they will seek to "deliver the goods". As this is a place of high energy output, planets here will draw on the energy of the other planets they aspect. This drains energy away from those areas of the chart. For example, a Sun in the stress zone before a cusp, and aspecting Saturn, might draw on the physical qualities of Saturnian energy in order to support its endeavours to assert itself and perform. This could lead to different forms of physical symptoms when the stress is felt.

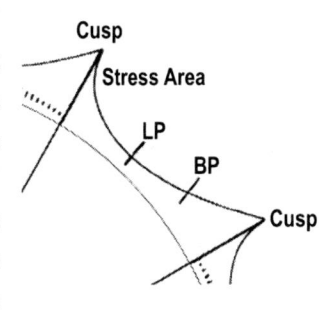

In the stress area there are feelings, via the planet concerned, of being far more interested in the matters of the upcoming house than the one the planet is actually placed in. There will be an impatience to act, an inability to rest. We will feel stirred to action and will urgently want to enter into the activities of the next house. A planet in the 2nd house but stressed before the 3rd will be far more interested in 3rd house matters and issues. In the stress zone of any house planets are likely to be more pushy, annoying, arrogant, feel frustrated in their efforts, competitive, in need of recognition and not easily controlled. Planets in the stress area are likely to "shout".

Things are somewhat different though when a planet is **on the cusp** of a house. Here planets will sing. They are more able to act decisively and without stress. However, as they are right on the cusp – the peak of the wave pattern – they are very much in the spotlight because the cusp is an external point of focus. Planets here can still be noisy, but in a far less aggressive, competitive way. They can put themselves out into the world in a more relaxed manner, rather like a jazz trumpeter who can coolly but confidently play his instrument with an air of having got it all together, but who also does not want to be ignored.

Approximately one third of the way through a house we find the **Balance Point**. This is where the energy coming from the inner core of the chart is at its optimum point of balance with the demands and expectations of the environment. Planets on a Balance Point can be expressed comfortably without tiring or draining the individual. They are more able to accomplish tasks efficiently. Here there is a sense of skill in action, an ease of expression and success out in the world.

Approximately two thirds of the way through a house the **Low Point** is reached. This corresponds to the troughs in the wave pattern, and planets placed here can be quiet and "whisper". As already mentioned, the psychological starting point of each house is the Low Point of the previous house, which is closest to the central core of the chart and the energy which flows from this place. The knack with Low Point planets is to remember that the energy comes from within, and it is this which must be responded to first, before the Low Point planet can begin to successfully express itself out in the world. Low Point planets can be a source of frustration as what they have to offer is not always recognised or wanted by the world. Their outward expression of energy can be difficult. If they are ignored then they tend to get noisy and kick up a fuss in order to be seen or heard; unfortunately such attempts at recognition often result in the world turning away from them even more.

Low Point planets can represent a part of us which was not allowed to develop fully or naturally when we were younger, so we have the option to go back and reclaim that part of ourselves, working on the developmental stages of that particular planet or drive. Low Point planets which are trained by having their energy channelled into specific tasks or activities can be used far more effectively out in the world. For example, a Low Point Mars might be reclaimed and trained by taking part in physical activities, sport, dance or assertiveness skills. A Low Point Mercury can be trained by keeping a diary, journal or blog, writing – but just for yourself – calligraphy, singing or voice training.

Connecting with the qualities and energies of Low Point planets can lead to greater spiritual awareness, because it is through these planets that we can eventually come to express and fulfil more of our life purpose. But we need to first get a "handle" on what the Low Point planets are really and truly all about for us. If we don't have any Low Point planets, it's possible that this lifetime is one of consolidation, rest, or learning other lessons. Low Point planets offer a place of inner stillness to be explored or ignored; if we choose to explore and embrace what it offers we will find this can be an enriching experience, rewarding on both inner and outer levels.

"What about planets that are not at any of these places in the Dynamic Curve?"

Of course there are always likely to be planets in a chart that don't fall on any of the positions described. Yet these planets will still reflect, in their output and expression, the energy of the Dynamic Curve. Assessing their position within it can be a useful indicator of the way they will behave, so they should also be considered in the chart as a whole.

Each house is divided into three distinct areas:

1. Cusp to Balance Point, which is the cardinal zone of the house. Planets in this area act and respond in an initiatory, proactive and outgoing manner. They are high-powered, with plenty of get-up-and-go.

2. Balance Point to Low Point, which is the fixed zone of the house. Planets here are quieter, more stable, conservative and less go-ahead. They seek to keep things as they are and resist change.

3. Low Point to Cusp, which is the mutable zone of the house. Planets in this area are more mobile and flexible, perhaps fluctuating in their output of energy and interaction with the environment. They want to move on and seek out new ground and have a quality of anticipation and excitement (and potential stress the closer they are to the cusp).

Example – Planetary Positions

This is the chart of a young man whose Age Point has just entered the 6th house. It provides some good examples of planets in different parts of the Dynamic Curve. Mercury, strong at 13°, is stressed before the DC. Moon, equally strong at 14°, is on the Balance Point in the 4th house. Venus, strongest of all at 11½° is on the Low Point in

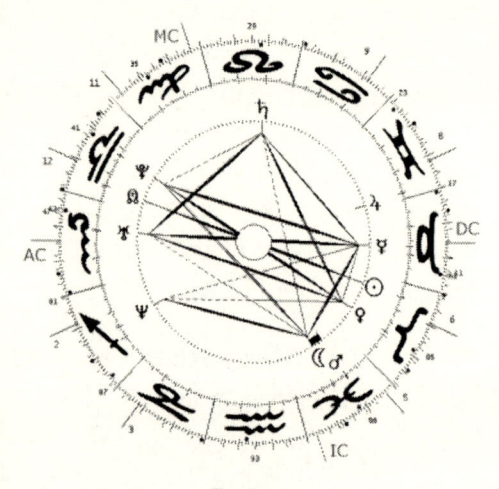

James
14.4.1977, 21:55, Leeds, UK

the 5th. This could be a potential source of conflict, particularly in the area of relationships, as the capacity to express Venus energies is strong but his ability to do so could be held back and prone to misunderstanding because it is on the Low Point. The Sun, weaker at almost 25°, is in the cardinal zone of the 6th house.

It is an interesting chart. The whole structure seems to be suspended from intercepted Saturn, the highest planet, as if from a hook or coat hanger, begging the question "What significance does security, structure and organisation have in his life?" This is especially relevant as Jupiter, which represents quite opposite qualities to Saturn, is unaspected in the 7th house. The shaping is a mixture of fixed and dynamic, giving a motivation that will sometimes seek stability, and at other times will be more flexible. Most of the green aspects are enclosed within those which are red/blue around the outside of the aspect structure, suggesting an inner sensitivity and perhaps a "prickliness" as well, as there is an incomplete Irritation rectangle spanning the 6/12 axis. The direction is a mixture of vertical and horizontal with strong-by-sign Mercury, the recipient of mainly red and green aspects, stressed and active before the DC.

Example – Low Point Planet

I have Mars on a Low Point, which makes it weak by house position. At 6° of Cancer, it is also relatively weak by sign. When I first discovered this feature in my own chart I was none too happy! The truth of the matter was that the features of a Low Point planet, and my experience of asserting myself using Mars, was all too close to home for comfort. I did not like what my chart was revealing because my behaviour was described to a 'T'. My Low Point Mars **was** prone to kicking up a fuss and trying very hard to make itself heard. And the more I used it in this way, the less successful the end result seemed to be.

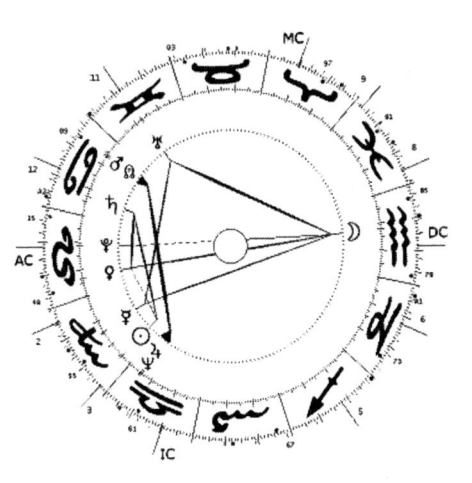

Joyce Hopewell
19.09.1945, 02:30, Tadcaster, UK

An example of this involved me buying some waterproof clothing for walking in. The label in the cagoule and over-trousers implied that both were waterproofed; the shop assistant confirmed that they were, so I bought them in preparation for a weekend trek up Snowdon, the highest mountain in Wales. Feeling smugly protected against anything the weather might bring, I set off in my new outerwear. It started to rain. The rain set in and was heavy and persistent. Clouds hung low over Snowdon and visibility dropped dangerously so there was no option but to turn back. It was then I noticed I was feeling not just damp, but wet. The so-called waterproofs were leaking through every seam.

On the Monday morning I took the offending outerwear back to the shop where I had bought it, along with my (as I imagined) very assertive Mars. I ranted and raved at the assistant, demanding to see the manager and demanding my money back. It all fell on deaf ears; the assistant was not in the least impressed or fazed and the manager turned out not to be in the shop until the following day. The more fuss I made, the less effect I seemed to have. I returned the next day with a valuable but humbling lesson under my belt; my Low Point Mars was not heard and I was not able to be assertive at all. Of course my money was returned but I then had to learn consciously how to assert myself using Mars. Skill, tactics and sometimes courage, too, have had to be called upon in order for me to successfully express my Low Point Mars in subsequent similar situations.

On the plus side, the Low Point position of my Mars means that I have easy access to an inner strength, stamina and courage which have stood me in good stead in various situations where it would have been preferable to take flight.

Example – Cuspal Planet

Penny's chart offers an interesting example. Her unaspected Sun is very strongly placed on the 3rd house cusp. Hers is a "You" sided, vertical chart with the majority of the planets in the lower hemisphere. This suggests an easy ability to tune in to the mood, ideas, feelings, concerns and interests of the collective. The Sun in Gemini is

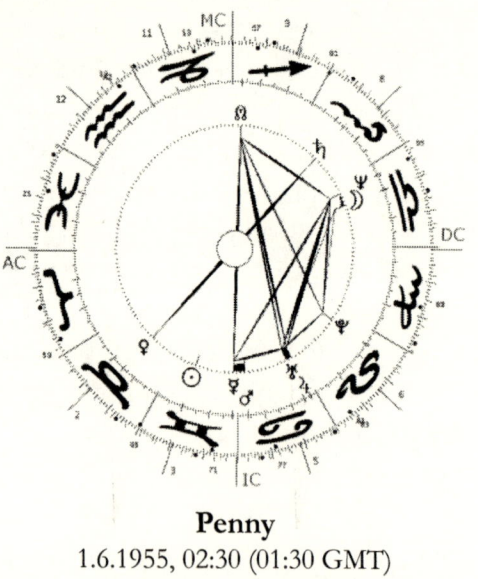

Penny
1.6.1955, 02:30 (01:30 GMT)
52.23 N, 001.43 W

strong by sign at 10°, and strong by house being on the cusp. Its Gemini qualities are likely to be reinforced as it is able to "sing" and be heard from this place on the 3rd cusp. However, being unaspected could be a blessing or a curse. Using her Gemini Sun,

Penny will be able to move out into the environment in pursuit of a variety of different and infinitely interesting snippets of information. Like a bloodhound, she can pick up the scent of some tantalising titbit, but she may fail, or simply forget to bring it back to base so that it can be evaluated. The distractions out there will be too great, and off she will go following another scent.

Penny offers this feedback:

"You are spot on about the unaspected Sun. The internet is fatal to a Sun like this, as there is always more information to seek! My biggest problem is harnessing the energy and pinning it down/applying it to one or two constructive activities. I have an almost overwhelming urge to keep on finding more and more out instead of going with what I have got. I quell this impulse now – when I can spot it. I do feel that I tune in quite easily to the collective... and found this really useful when teaching teenagers because I could angle the material in a way that grabbed their attention. I was teaching information technology – very Gemini! I am widely read but my reading has tended to be extensive rather than intensive. I am actually working on my reading style now – focusing down and reading single texts very carefully rather than many texts superficially.

With this strong but sometimes 'rogue' Sun I have to pull in the troops from somewhere else in my chart. Looking back at when I was studying for my degree I really feel that I looked for Saturnine strengths to support my Sun. I knew I needed to bring in a steadying influence that had focus on practicality. This awareness helped me confine my reading and research to the task at hand... getting the degree rather than reading and gathering more and more information. Which brings me to willpower... when I harness that energy (and ignore distraction) I have immense will and drive to succeed in any task I set myself. This probably is helped by the strong position of the Sun."

Innate Qualities and Environment

Sign and House Strength

In Chapter 3 we have already considered the potential conflict between our innate qualities and the environment, as reflected in the strength of an ego planet by sign (innate) and by house (environment). Similar analysis can be applied to each of the planets and their strength by sign and by house. Here we are going to focus on the Dynamic Calculations, which give an aggregate measure across the whole chart.

The Dynamic Calculations

	Total	Crosses - Motivation			Elements - Temperament			
		Car	Fix	Mut	Fire	Earth	Air	Water
Signs	100	55	21	24	7	32	35	26
House	143	81	48	14	44	0	33	66
Diff.	43	26	27	-10	37	-32	-2	40

"What do those numbers in the boxes mean?"

The boxes – the Dynamic Calculations – appear on Huber-specific computer data and on hand-drawn chart forms. They offer information about innate qualities and the conditioning and influences that the individual has received from the environment and upbringing.

The Dynamic Calculations relate to what we bring into this life inherently by sign – our inherited attributes, talents and qualities. The Dynamic Calculations can show how these attributes have been either over- or under-formed by the conditioning we received as we were growing up and the expectations which were laid upon us by the environment. This relates specifically to the houses, so what we're looking at when we decipher the figures in the boxes is a combination of our nature and nurture, and the interaction of our heredity and environment, of which we are a product.

"How do you start working with the figures?"

The first and most important thing to do is check if the time of birth you are working with is accurate. If it is not, then what the Dynamic Calculations will tell you is not reliable. A scoring system is used to arrive at the figures used in the Dynamic Calculations, based on the placement of the planets by sign and house. Each planet is scored differently according to its position, and different weightings are given to each planet. The Dynamic Calculations are normally worked out by the Huber software used, but it is possible (although not necessarily desirable!) to calculate them manually. However, what is of most interest to us is their **interpretation**, and understanding what they show. You are recommended to refer back to the Dynamic Calculation boxes shown at the beginning of this section, or preferably, if you are working with your own Dynamic Calculations, to have these in front of you.

The Stress Total

What is known as the Stress Total is found in the first column, at the bottom left-hand corner (+43 in the example opposite). This figure shows the overall stress score, and it is useful to consider this first when starting to interpret the Dynamic Calculations.

"What do you mean by 'stress'?"

You are probably aware of what stress is from your own life experience because without a doubt we all become stressed at times. A dictionary definition of stress might say it is something like "a constraining, impelling force, where effort is required and there are great demands made upon energy." Likewise, the Stress Total in the Dynamic Calculations shows the overall stress score which reflects the general amount of stress and strain we experience in life generally. This comes in the form of the push, the expectations, the squeezing in of everything in a busy life and the urgency felt to meet deadlines. We all need some stress in our lives. Too much and we get overloaded and become ill;

too little and we become inert and passive. The ideal is to be somewhere between these two extremes, and it's here that the figures can offer information about the comparative intensity of these stress levels.

"A plus or a minus?"

Plus scores have a "comfort zone" range of between +5 and +25. If, for example, the overall stress score shown in the Dynamic Calculations in the bottom left hand box is +14, that falls within this range and is not likely to be experienced as unduly excessive or uncomfortable for the individual concerned.

If the score is above +25 pressures may be felt building up and the individual may feel less comfortable the higher the score is. Generally speaking, the higher the score, the more pressure and stress we are likely to experience, and that may be because of expectations which were placed upon us by the environment during our childhood or upbringing. A plus total indicates strong demands made on our inner resources by the outside world, and as a general rule of thumb, the higher the plus score, the greater the stress. We will be looking at the significance of high stress scores later in this section.

Minus scores, on the other hand, suggest that the person has much more free space available to be "looser" and to move unrestrained in any direction they want as they have an untapped well of resources and energy within. But with a minus score the person may feel the world isn't considering or recognising their talents and abilities; they might feel frustrated, misunderstood or unacknowledged, and could be seen as a bit of a black sheep. They may just switch off and not bother to make any efforts, feeling that no-one will recognise or welcome their talents and attributes and what they have to offer. An overall stress score in the Stress Total box which falls below +5 is already veering towards the minus status, so if you have a low plus score here, you may resonate to the minus score description.

The Signs and the Boxes on Line 1

The signs show the inherited traits we bring with us and their scores are listed under the headings "Motivation" – Cardinal, Fixed and Mutable, and "Temperament" – Fire, Earth, Air and Water. These scores are added across and both sets should add up to the same figures as that listed under the Stress Total column for the signs. Check this out now using your own Dynamic Calculations. Using these scores in this way is the best approach to gaining more understanding and familiarity with them.

The Houses and the Boxes on Line 2

The houses represent the outside world and the environmental conditioning which is imposed upon us, and which seeks to modify the inherent traits we bring to life with us. House scores are likewise listed under the same headings of "Motivation" and "Temperament" and their scores should come to the same figures in the Stress Total column when added up. Conflict can arise when there is an incompatibility between sign and house scores.

"How do I interpret these figures?"

Refer now to your own Dynamic Calculations (or if you don't have a print out of these, to the example calculations shown at the start of this section.) Line 1 shows the inherited sign qualities and characteristics numerically, the highest figures showing those that will predominate. In the example Dynamic Calculations figures, Line 1 under Cardinal scores +55 as the highest figure in the Motivation section, with Air scoring +35 as the highest under Temperament. This suggests that the person will inherently have plenty of cardinal and airy characteristics. They may have strong ideas or outspoken opinions, which they would like to express and they have the potential to be a forceful communicator, with assertive points of view. However, these traits will be modified by the expectation and demands of the environment, which may not have welcomed some of these traits.

Line 2 shows totals which relate to the houses, the areas of life experience and expression where expectations for us to "perform" are at their greatest. In the example figures, Line 2 under Cardinal scores +81 as the highest figure in the Motivation section, with Water scoring +66 as the highest under Temperament. This indicates that with such high scores for cardinal and water, the person is likely to have been conditioned in childhood to focus very strongly on expressing feelings rather than their inherent airy ideas and views. The environment probably focussed on encouraging these traits to the detriment of the naturally inherited cardinal/airy ones.

Exercise – Sign and House Scores

See now if you can you relate this to the figures in Lines 1 and 2 using your own Dynamic Calculations. What are your highest scores here, and what does this mean for you in the context of your own life? Make some notes for yourself on this.

Pluses and Minuses and the Boxes on Line 3

Line 3 show the totals arrived at after subtracting the sign scores (the inherited traits and characteristics, those which we bring with us) from the house scores (what the environment expects and demands from us). We subtract what we've brought with us from what the environment demanded and see how much we have left. It is Line 3 that we look at to give us, at a glance, the essential information needed to interpret these figures as a whole.

For example, using the figures in Line 3 under Motivation, the highest score is +27 in the Fixed column, and the highest score under Temperament on Line 3 is +40 in the Water column. Taken together, these give high scores for both Fixed and Water, indicating that the person could have been pushed by the environment into displaying these traits. They would have been encouraged to have steady, possibly inflexible emotional reactions and to consistently maintain the manner in which these were expressed. When plus scores are on the high side, the person is **over-formed** by the environment in these particular traits and qualities.

We then look to see what the lowest scores are on Line 3. Some of these may be minus scores, although this doesn't always happen. In the example we're using here, the lowest score under Motivation is -10 in the Mutable column, and under Temperament is -32 in the Earth column. Taken together this gives a low score for Mutable Earth qualities and tells us that the person has <u>more</u> of these qualities than the environment wants or is interested in. There is a surplus to requirement. Maybe these qualities were not approved of or encouraged during childhood so were ignored, not rewarded or were even punished in some way. When minus scores are found on Line 3, the person is **under-formed** by the environment in these particular traits and qualities.

Exercise – Plus and Minus Totals (1)

Take a look at your own Dynamic Calculations again, and consider the areas where you have high plus or minus scores. Make some notes about any over-forming or under-forming that you find, and relate this specifically to your life experience.

"Can you say more about high and low scores in the Stress Total box and on Line 3?"

Yes – we will return to this as stated earlier. A general rule of thumb was given: the higher the plus score, the greater the stress. To recap, the plus scores have a comfort zone of between +5 and +25, and generally speaking, the higher the plus score, the greater the amount of stress and expectation from the environment that the individual will "perform".

High Scores

However, if the plus score in the Stress Total column gets very high, say into the upper +40's or +50's, the stress will increase correspondingly. But if it then becomes exceptionally high and goes into the +60's or even +70's, the person concerned will probably not experience stress as they will be way above and beyond this. They will instead have a somewhat materialistic outlook on life where all their energy is channelled towards survival and achievement. They will adapt the environment to suit themselves. Generally speaking, such people are often successful but are relatively unaware of themselves, so they are unlikely to be interested in personal growth or self-awareness.

The +43 score in the sample Dynamic Calculations used in this section is a relevant example here. The score is quite high so stress is almost certainly going to be felt.

Example – Margaret Thatcher

The Dynamic Calculations for former British Prime Minister Margaret Thatcher (next page) show an overall stress score of +71. This is high, and at a level at which she would not have experienced stress, but would be more concerned with getting on with the job in hand, surviving and adapting the environment to suit herself. It's interesting to see that Margaret Thatcher has two zero scores in Line 3 of her Dynamic Calculations. These are in the Cardinal and Air columns. Bruno Huber observed that with a zero in Line 3, there is no push felt from the surroundings

		Crosses - Motivation			Elements - Temperament			
	Total	Car	Fix	Mut	Fire	Earth	Air	Water
Signs	101	51	36	14	24	11	31	35
House	172	51	31	90	64	28	31	49
Diff.	71	0	-5	76	40	17	0	14

Dynamic Calculations for Margaret Thatcher
13.10.1925, 09:00, Grantham, England

on this particular quality – in Mrs. Thatcher's case no push for either cardinal or air – and the quality is just accepted by the environment.

Low Scores

As we have already learned, minus scores start with figures below +5, and the stress increases as the minus scores get higher (for example, -13 would be getting high). Bruno Huber found that scores below +10 indicated awareness, and little sign of stress, but that there could be weakness. Minus scores indicate that the energy brought by inheritance (sign) is greater than the environment requires, so there is a surplus of untapped, unused and unrecognised energy. With minus scores the person has something to offer but the world does not want it, or maybe does not see or recognise it. Bruno Huber suggested that the person with minus scores may appear "cool", doing things the best they can, but at the same time they might be trying to avoid them. With minus numbers the person has to teach themselves to develop the relevant quality for its own sake, and not for the sake of pleasing others.

A minus score in the Stress Total column can indicate a repression or a neglect of talents and abilities. This can be frustrating as the person may feel misunderstood. But once they understand what is going on, the surplus energy can be harnessed, redirected and put to use.

Exercise – Plus and Minus Totals (2)

Spend some time now with your own Dynamic Calculations, looking for a combination under the Motivation and Temperament boxes for the two <u>highest</u> and the two <u>lowest</u> scores, and make some notes for yourself on this, based on your own life experience.

Look at the figures in your boxes and choose

- One high figure from Line 3 – either a plus or a minus score – from <u>either</u> the Motivation section (Cardinal, Fixed, Mutable) or the Temperament section (Fire, Earth, Air, Water)
- Connect with your feelings and experiences of this. Allow an image to arise which relates to a real life situation you've had when you were aware of a response from the environment to the under-forming or over-forming involved.
- Find a way of representing how this felt for you in any way you want – you could draw, use words, show it in colours, shapes etc. Express this in whichever way best captures this under-forming or over-forming for you.

The House Chart and Environmental Influences

The House chart can give many important and helpful insights into the nature of the environmental conditioning we received as a child. It offers a key to understanding how, and in which areas of life, we have been conditioned as it can reveal how our nature has been affected by the nurture we received. This may be experienced by us as either positive or negative. However we might have experienced our upbringing, the significant fact remains that when working with the House chart, we can **choose** whether or not we use our inherited potential (as found in the natal chart) or our conditioned potential (as found in the house chart), or whether we want to live creatively, combining elements from both charts.

"What is the House Chart?"

Whereas the natal chart shows our potential and the inherited patterns of intention and purpose that we are born with, the house chart represents our conditioned behaviour patterns. It reflects the expectations of our surrounding environment and the conditioning we received when we were children.

The house chart is our "start up" equipment for life. We are born into a specific family and environment, and as children we grow up, taking on and responding to the expectations and conditioning of that environment. The house chart provides the **ingredients and potential** for moving forward from birth, incorporating those inherited traits and potential with the taught and conditioned traits and behaviours we learn from our environment. In view of this it is important to remember that, as children, we need to respond to our environment and the influences within in order to survive.

The house chart can appear very different to the natal chart, and the visual impact of any differences is the first thing to consider when looking at it. A general rule of thumb is that the greater the difference between the natal and house chart, the greater the conditioning the individual will have received.

If you have copies of your own natal and house charts you might like to put them alongside each other now and look to see if there are visual differences between them. Opposite are three examples of natal and house charts. You can see how visually the two charts of these three people differ considerably.

"How is the House Chart set up?"

Exactly the same data is used for the house chart as for the natal chart, but the viewpoint taken is different. The house chart views the individual in an objective way, whereas the natal chart has a subjective viewpoint. Using the house chart, the individual is the person as seen from the outside, looking in. It represents the way the world looks at the person rather than the way person looks at the world, so it contains all the assumptions, set conditions and cultural expectations that the outside world might have for that person.

The spaces allocated to the signs and houses change places. The signs become distorted and lose their 30 degree size; the houses instead are all 30 degrees in size. The signs are either bigger or smaller, giving clues as to which of the basic archetypes show more or less. Some may be enlarged and appear to be spread more thinly; others may shrink and appear condensed, but this might also have an intensifying effect. This could be especially significant if there are planets positioned in them.

"How do I start to look at the two charts?"

- **Important**: always look at the two charts **together**; do not consider the house chart in isolation.
- Approach your interpretation in the same way as you would with the natal chart.
- Find an intuitive image for the chart – does it resonate with the natal chart or is it quite different?
- Consider the colour, shaping, motivation, direction of the chart.
- Using the two charts alongside you can begin to compare nature and nurture – the individual is a product of the environment.

4. *Integrating with the Environment* 105

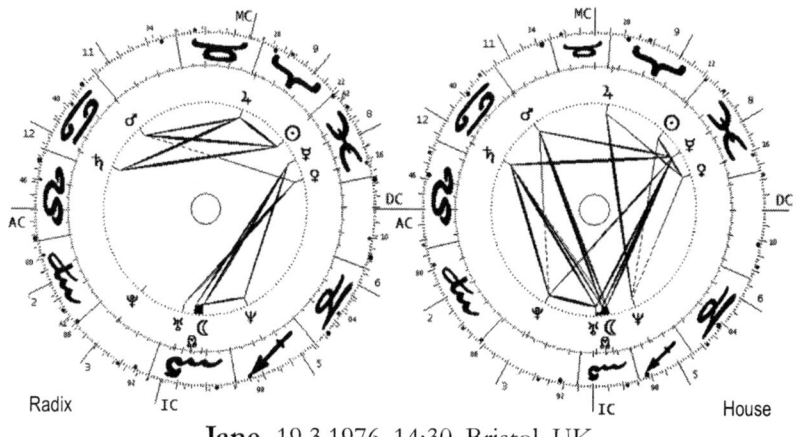

Radix | IC | House
Jane 19.3.1976, 14:30, Bristol, UK

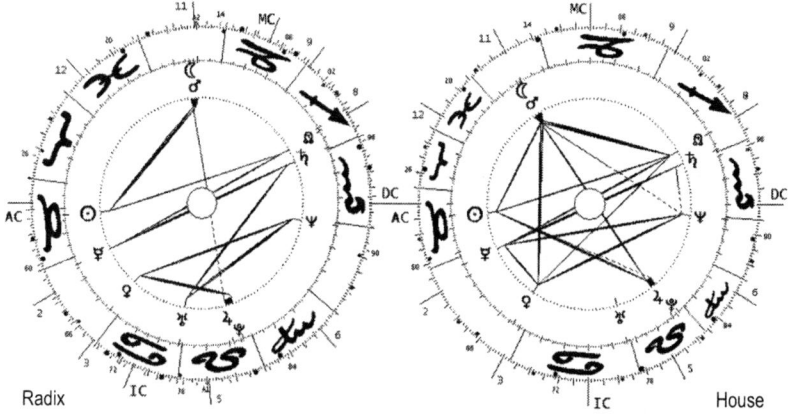

Radix | IC | House
Chart D 3.5.1956, 05:30 (04:30 GMT), 53.25 N, 002.55 W

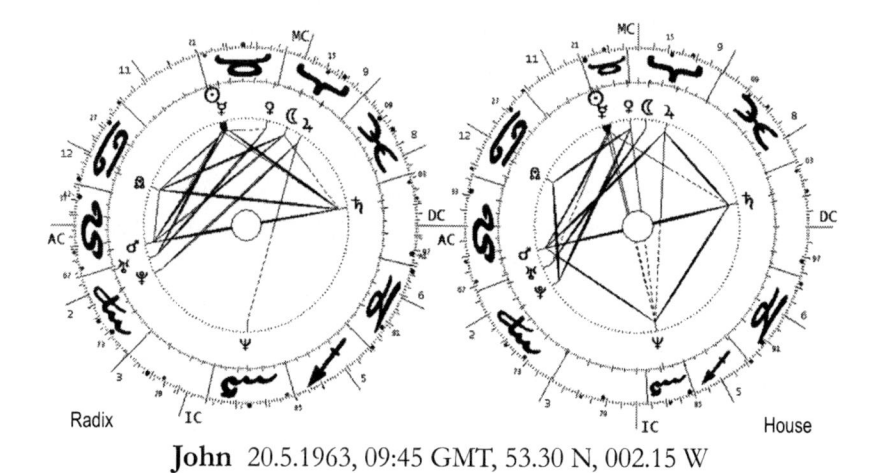

Radix | IC | House
John 20.5.1963, 09:45 GMT, 53.30 N, 002.15 W

Natal and House Chart Examples

- Remember **H**eredity x **E**nvironment = the **I**ndividual: **H** x **E** = **I**.
- With the House chart you are looking at traits that have been taught rather than those that have been inherited.

"What does the House Chart show?"

The house chart shows what the world tried to make of us in our formative years. It contains the influences, expectations and conditioning that were laid upon us during our early years. This would have come directly from family, friends, teachers and the community we grew up in. The influence of this conditioning is likely to remain with us until we are well into our teens and until we begin to assert ourselves using the qualities inherent in our natal chart.

As well as indicating the expectations laid upon us, the house chart can be seen as our potential **future**, too, as it contains all that is built into us during childhood. Depending on how we use and value what we learned and were conditioned into as children, we may as adults either choose to keep what is of use to us, or discard the unwanted conditioning and go our own way. The conditioning we receive is not necessarily wrong; it may simply be wrong for us as we pursue our individual paths of personal growth and self-awareness. Alternatively, we could easily discover that the expectations from the environment which we disliked having put upon us as children have reasonable benefits for us in adult life. You could take the viewpoint that we ourselves choose to be born into a particular family environment, so the influences we receive are beneficial. Once we've found their meaning we can consciously choose which traits we wish to retain, and which we want to dump.

By the time the mid-teens are reached, young people can feel that they are what the environment has educated them to be. The values and attitudes learned from the house chart begin to weaken as the person gains a growing realisation of who they really are and what they feel themselves to really be. The potential of the natal chart is awakened and they start to grow into it. If there is a big difference between the natal and house charts, there will be a period of discomfort and upheaval as the young person seeks to discover their identity. Teenage years may be edgy and turbulent, with rebellious behaviour and a general kicking back against the expectations of the environment. This will manifest through behaviour, dress, language, choice of music and friends and taste in general. If there is a smaller difference this experience will be reduced and any adjustments will be easier and less fraught.

"How does this work, though, if the Natal Chart is a difficult and challenging one?"

Using the Huber Method, we tend not to class charts as "difficult" or act like garage mechanics sucking in their breath and slowly shaking our heads. Charts can be challenging, there is no denying this. A natal chart with such features may well have a house chart which shows potentially very beneficial conditioning from the environment. However, the person may be strongly pulled to experience the difficult pattern in the natal chart, and be unaware that there are alternative ways out of this. If we are working on the charts of family and friends, and come across this kind of situation we can show them that there is an alternative to be found in the house chart. A doorway can be opened for them to acknowledge and own the benefits that the environment has offered them and it can be very helpful for the person to be shown these alternatives. We can point them towards the good things their environment and conditioning has offered. In my own experience, this did happen with a client who came for a session. She knew nothing about astrology, but took one look at her natal chart and said "That's a really awful birth chart." Yes, it was a challenging chart, but it was softened, tempered and modified by what the house chart had to offer. But only she could choose this option for herself instead of remaining stuck with the 'awful' birth chart.

A very red/green natal chart may become a very blue/green house chart. The red/green indicates an excess of sensitivity, making the person touchy and prickly and perhaps difficult to get along with. The blue/green of the house chart would suggest that the conditioning received would have had a softening effect with the environment encouraging them to be a more harmonious person who is easier to live with.

"How do I work with the Natal and House Charts together?"

The golden rule is to never use the house chart on its own because if used alone it will give a one-sided view of the person and will miss out on important essentials; always use it alongside the natal chart.

Firstly
- Compare house and natal charts by looking at them using your eyes and senses. Are there differences in the chart image? Or changes in the shaping and motivation?
- Look at the number of aspects and their colours. Does the ratio change? If it does, what might this mean?
- Is there a *reduction* or an *enhancement* from the natal to the house chart in terms of more or less aspects? If the number of aspects has been enriched because there are more in the house chart, then the person will have been enriched by the conditioning they received. They will have gained additional equipment for life. That can be beneficial as it can offer more opportunities.
- Use what you already know and understand about colours of aspects. An increase in the number of blue aspects gives more ease, more rest, especially in a very red natal chart; an increase in green may hint at clever "brainy" surroundings and conditioning as green aspects are those of consciousness.
- If the house chart aspects have been reduced, then the person has been reduced. This may be good if the reduction has the effect of making the overall structure and appearance of the chart clearer and more focussed. A reduction indicates that some of the person's abilities were not wanted by the environment – perhaps they were too noisy or too strong. When working with charts which show a reduction, be aware

that this is not always easy to take on board and that the person could feel that they have been repressed, pushed down and generally not accepted. When working with charts showing a reduction, treat the person concerned (and it may be you) with sensitivity.

Secondly
- Look at the space filled in both charts. This may appear either more or less ordered, and this in itself can tell you something.

Thirdly
- Note if any of the single aspects are different – a trine in the natal chart might become a square in the house chart. A trine in the natal chart gives more ease; if it changes to a square in the house chart there will be more tension and working energy involved.
- Take into consideration any changes involved in the planets making the aspects.

Fourthly
- Look to see if any new aspect patterns have appeared in the house chart. Triangular or quadrilateral figures which are not present in the natal chart may appear.
- Check to see if there are any unaspected planets in the house chart which are integrated in the natal chart. If a planet is unaspected in the house chart, it may be that the environment didn't want to know about it, was not interested in it, ignored it and simply left it out. For example, an unaspected Venus in the house chart may relate to the child who did drawings or paintings which the environment wasn't interested in. Instead of them being admired and put on the wall, they would have been put in the bin. Conversely, an unaspected planet in the natal chart which is integrated in the house chart can indicate the environment's inclusion and recognition of the qualities associated with that planet.

Example – House Chart

When working with the Huber Method, it is customary for the teacher to use their own chart as an example to illustrate the topic being taught. This is because we are working with real life experiences in astrological psychology, and are best able to speak our own truth if we base what is said on what has been experienced and understood first hand. For this reason I am using my own natal and house charts (facing page) to illustrate some of the points raised in this section.

Although there are not a large number of changes between the two charts, the clarity and relative simplicity of the overall aspect pattern assist in making it easy to see the differences.

Visual image – this is similar in both charts. The racing yacht tipped on its side, keel below the water, which I described in Chapter 1 is still tipped at an uncomfortable angle, but the keel is larger, giving a greater sense of stability. The large sail is still billowing in the wind, but its direction has changed, as if the boom it is attached to has swung round. Maybe there has been a change in the wind direction!

Chart shaping/motivation – both charts are predominantly dynamic with some linear motivation. There is no big discrepancy here, such as might be felt if the shaping of the natal chart was predominantly linear, and that of the house chart was fixed.

Colour ratio – there is quite a change here. My natal chart has 5 red : 3 green : 2 blue aspects, whereas my house chart has 4 red : 1 green : 5 blue. I lose red and green aspects and gain more blue, which I lack in my natal chart. What this means to me in the context of my charts **and** in the context of my real life experience is that the environment and the conditioning I received played down my red "doing" energy and motivation. It encouraged me to be more blue, more stable, less active and to have a greater tendency to take rest, be more relaxed and less urgently interested in being busy or going off to do something.

4. Integrating with the Environment 111

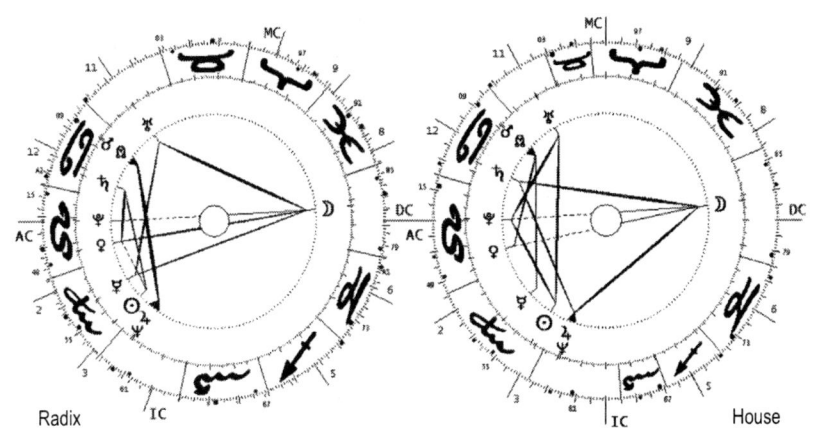

Joyce Hopewell Natal and House Charts
19.09.1945, 02:30, Tadcaster, UK

Enriching or diminishing? – I have to be totally honest here and say that gaining more blue from my house chart is an enriching gift for me. Without it I would probably become overworked, not know when to stop and would get ill. But I have to work at remembering I have the potential and ability to balance out my inherent "redness" and tendency to extreme activity with my conditioned "blueness" and ability to ease off and enjoy. I can only access the blue when I do so consciously, making it my choice to behave in this way.

Cohesion and the space filled in both charts – again, there are similarities between the two charts. The most noticeable difference is in the way the lower hemisphere of the house chart appears to have a greater focus because of the orientation of the aspect patterns. Belonging to the collective and "fitting in" was encouraged above being an individual and "different".

Differences in the aspects – the natal chart quincunx from Moon to Mercury disappears, but a quincunx between Moon and Saturn appears in the house chart. This relates directly to the Family Model and the relationship between my mother and myself as I was growing up. This was not always easy and could be edgy as we both vied for the position of "top dog." A quincunx between Family Model planets can show that a relationship existed where the parameters were not clear.

Changes in aspect patterns – I lose the Ear/Eye or Information triangle in the natal chart. Although I have no conscious memory of the attributes of this aspect pattern being discouraged, not required or ignored, I can see how the change of direction and pinning planets in the Dominant Learning triangle might have contributed to a lack of recognition of the Ear/Eye.

The Dominant Learning triangle takes on a different combination of planets. Instead if being a direct triangle with Uranus, Mercury, Moon, it becomes, in the house chart, a retrograde triangle with Jupiter/Neptune, Saturn, Moon. Messages I associate with this retrograde learning figure are "Keep plodding on", "Try your hardest" and "If at first you don't succeed, try, try again." It was as if my environment didn't expect me to get things right, or understand them first time around when in fact I often did! Saturn is involved in this retrograde figure and these messages most often came from my mother.

What I gain is a Small Talent triangle. This figure includes the Sun, and it was my father who encouraged me to develop myself. The messages included "Be able to do something that will make you popular and always in demand", "Learn a skill – play the piano, learn to play tennis". I did some of those things but in adult years have been able to draw upon my potential to develop my own "talent" by developing my understanding of astrological psychology.

We may, at some stage in life, have to live by the house chart and through the patterns of behaviour by which we have been conditioned. But we can swap between this and our natal chart and with awareness we can learn to draw on the attributes of both charts, utilising that which is more beneficial to us. We have to do this consciously, and the amount of freedom we have to move from one to the other depends on how developed our personal awareness is and how we are exercising our ability to choose and create our own lives.

Chapter 5

Reconciling Past, Present and Future

Using The Three Charts

In the Huber Method three charts are used: the Natal chart, which shows the traits, characteristics and potential with which we are born into this world, the Moon Node chart, which we will be focussing on and working with in this chapter, and the House chart, described in the last chapter, which can reveal our conditioning and the environmental influences and expectations which have been brought to bear upon us.

Used together, these three charts can offer a rounded and in-depth picture of the whole person, showing where they have come from (in the moon node chart), where they are now (in the natal chart) and where they are going (in the house chart.) Bruno Huber spoke of the house chart as being the chart of the future, and by this he meant the future that we **create for ourselves**, based on the conditioning and experiences that we have had during our formative years, combined with the potential contained in the natal chart. This chart can be used, alongside the natal chart, as a way of helping us move towards the next step on our own path of personal growth.

Moon Node and Natal Charts

The Moon Node chart is unique to the Huber Method and plays an important role in the holistic approach used in astrological psychology. It can be likened to a mirror: we can look into it to discover more about the shadow side of the personality, and it can reveal the accumulated knowledge and experience we bring with us to this lifetime. The moon node chart is always used alongside the natal chart, and can be a valuable tool on the path of self discovery and understanding because it can reveal where we come from, along with some of our familiar habitual patterns of response. We may choose to leave some of these behind, once we are able to see them for what they are.

"What is the psychological meaning of the Moon Node chart?"

Psychologically the node chart can help to make the shadow side of the personality visible. It represents that part of ourselves which contains the repressed drives, motivations, projections, habitual traits and responses that exist at the unconscious level. It is these which can lead to compulsive behaviour. The shadow will contain things that we do not like about ourselves, things we may push down, deny or project onto others. When the shadow is repressed it does not go away but instead appears in our environment and surroundings as projections. Events and experiences mirror back to us the very things we are repressing in ourselves.

"What is the esoteric/karmic meaning of the Moon Node chart?"

Taken from a more esoteric point of view, the node chart can be likened to a store of all the accumulated "know how" we have brought into this lifetime. It contains the sum total of all past life experiences but it is important to recognise that what is there **does not** relate to specific events or specific lifetimes. It does, however, show accumulated skills, knowledge, information gained, and familiar, well-used behaviour patterns which we tend to fall back upon. As such it will indicate our cosy, familiar, habitual responses and reveal where and how we feel comfortable and at ease. For the most part, this behaviour will be unconscious until we bring it into our own conscious awareness. When we look at the node chart and seek to understand it we are dealing with the astral level, which is built around feelings and desires, battles and conflict. In order for us not to be drawn into this feeling level of the chart it is essential that we are clear, harmless and most of all, non-judgemental, when we use this chart for ourselves or for others.

When taking this particular view of the node chart, we can see that it is essentially concerned with our desire nature, which in esoteric terms relates to the astral body. The chart is constructed around the Moon, which is associated with our emotional needs and having these met. Because of this, the moon node chart can hold us back and keep us from moving forwards, especially when these needs are involved. We often react as if blindfolded and with little or no awareness that we are coming purely from an emotionally needy place.

It is certainly not wrong to have emotional needs, but it is very useful to be aware for ourselves of where we are coming from when we seek to have them met. They can be the prime cause of many of the problems and challenges we encounter in life, especially in the area of relationships. The node chart can give us clues as to how we go about getting our desires satisfied. We could even be driven by them to the extent of identifying **more** with the behaviour patterns found in the node chart than we are by what is in the natal chart. We may, in fact, be living life as if we're looking backwards over our shoulders through our own doorway in time rather than looking ahead to where we could be going.

The Hubers describe the moon node chart as an illusion – something that is no longer there – and as a mirror sphere where the desires, wishes, projections and motivations from the past are accumulated. They write about this chart in depth in *Moon Node Astrology*, so for the purposes of this book only a brief overview of the node chart is included as a preamble to the practical exercises included in this chapter for working with this chart.

"How is the Moon Node chart set up?"

This is detailed in *Moon Node Astrology* and in the API (UK) Diploma Course, and is summarised briefly here:

- It is based on the natal chart and is always used alongside this, never on its own.
- The North Node in the natal chart becomes the AC in the moon node chart; the natal AC becomes the North Node in the moon node chart. In most instances, the North Node appears in the same house in both charts.
- The signs are drawn in a clockwise direction, making the node chart appear as a mirror image when placed alongside the natal chart.
- The Equal House system is used in the node chart (i.e. 30° per house) and the houses are interpreted more along the lines of conventional/traditional astrology, as the node chart is concerned with what is past.

"What should I bear in mind when looking at the Moon Node chart?"

We have to remember that our environment and surroundings hold up a mirror to us, and when looking into the moon node chart we need to be aware that it, too, is just like a mirror. What it shows is not really there, is not real. The chart shows a reflection of the past, of where we've come from, or of our shadow side. If we explore it in depth we could unearth some things about ourselves that we don't like or don't approve of. We might be tempted to feel guilty about what we consider, from the perspective of where we are **now**, as distasteful or unacceptable. So it is important to remember that we are looking at this chart from a historical perspective where the evolution of human consciousness was not as advanced as it is now. From an evolutionary viewpoint, whatever it is that you discover about yourself when working with this chart, you can remind yourself that everything that you might have done took place in the past. All the chart is doing is acting as a mirror, and what it reveals is not real right here and now. Anything discovered in this chart must be set against a historical background, and in the context of time past, when values and attitudes were different from those held today.

The most important thing to bear in mind is to be **clear and harmless** when working with the moon node chart. Make no judgements, make no blame. Be discriminative in your thinking and approach the chart from the level of the mind. Do not make any statements about the chart or what you see in it based on your feelings. It is important to stay clear in this way because it is then possible to look at your own node chart, and the charts of others, and to accept and own what you see there. If you look for the karma and the guilt, that is what you will find, but if you look positively for what is good in this chart it can become an aid in your personal integration and synthesis.

"How do I interpret the Moon Node chart?"

As the moon node chart shows the sum total of all you have learned and experienced in previous incarnations and the nature of your shadow side, and the natal chart shows what you have come to learn about and experience in this lifetime, then it is important that you always look at these two charts together. The recommended way of doing this is to place the node chart to the left, and the natal chart to the right. The houses in the node chart are interpreted traditionally, because this chart relates to the past, and to times gone by. For example, when interpreted traditionally, the 12th house in this chart will stand for institutions, isolation, and withdrawal from society, perhaps through imprisonment, hospitalisation, monastic life etc.

118   The Living Birth Chart

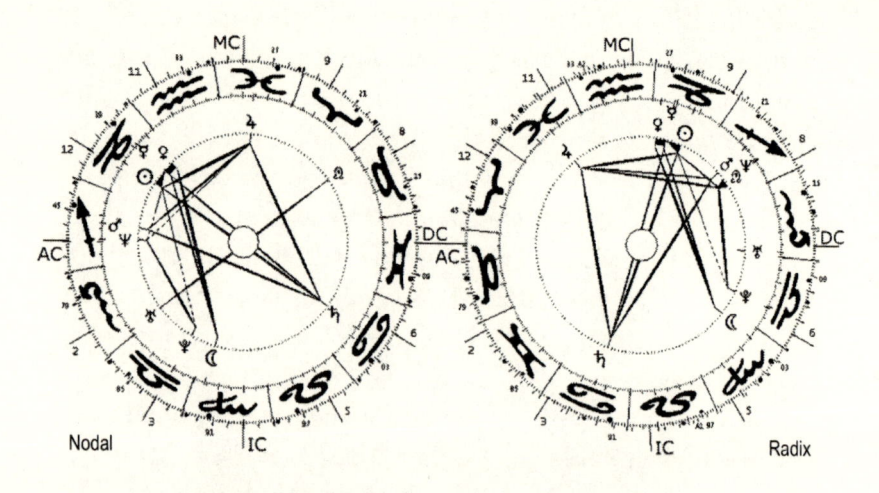

Nodal   IC   IC   Radix

Lorna – Moon Node and Natal Charts
03.01.1975, 13:45 (11:45 GMT), 29.49 S, 031.01 E

The moon node and natal charts for Lorna show the commonly seen mirroring effect between the two charts.

Many people tend to live out what is shown in their node chart and are not fully activating or exploring the potential of their natal chart. We all do this from time to time, so it is useful to be aware of it. But can you suggest **why** people might live in the moon node chart? The answer is that it is probably easier to respond to the demands of life from a place of familiarity – remember, the node chart is cosy but offers no growth. If we respond from this chart we do not have to grow and change and we stay on familiar territory. This might be especially so if we find that the present circumstances we are in are too much of a struggle to cope with. Then we will hanker for the past and respond in ways that are habitual. It is always more testing to find new ways of dealing with challenging situations, and to do this we have to activate the potential and learn the lessons of the natal chart.

Exercise – Interpreting the Moon Node Chart

It is suggested that you use your own moon node and natal charts for this exercise, laying them out alongside each other as those shown opposite.

Begin your comparison of the two charts using exactly the same approach as you would for looking at the natal chart. Consider the following points in your node chart:

- The intuitive image or chart picture
- Colour balance
- Overall chart shaping and motivation
- Direction of aspects
- I/You sided emphasis
- Quadrant emphasis (this is covered in *The Cosmic Egg Timer* and in the API (UK) Diploma Course)

As you take each point in turn, compare your findings with what is in the natal chart and note any significant changes, making notes for yourself on these.

Ego Planets in Moon Node and Natal Charts

Consideration of the three ego planets (Sun, Moon and Saturn) and their changes of position by house from the moon node chart to the natal chart will give clues as to how the personality, via body, feelings and mind, might be operating in both charts.

☉ Sun

The house where the Sun is found in the node chart will indicate an area of life expression which is already familiar. Here we will already know how and where to express ourselves using the mind, the decision-making processes or the will. Our sense of self will already be strong in this area. It could also be where we assert our power and authority, and where we seek status and standing, demanding recognition from the world around us.

☽ Moon

The Moon's house placement in the node chart will show our dependencies and what kind of people or contacts we may have sought out (and perhaps still do seek out) in order to feel looked after, loved and cared for. The house and the range of life experiences associated with it will describe our emotional needs, how we could still, in our everyday life, go about having these met, and in which area of life we will seek to have them fulfilled.

♄ Saturn

The position of Saturn by house will reveal our expectations and all our attitudes which have a "taken for granted" quality to them. Saturn symbolises form of all kinds, and that includes thought forms, ideas and maybe dogma, too, if Saturn is in an air house (for example the 3rd). Saturn will show where we habitually look for our ideas, rules or guidelines. It will indicate where we seek frameworks to help structure our thoughts, and will offer clues as to what these might be. Thoughts, attitudes and ideas could be crystallised and rigid; we are inclined to cling on to these well-known structures like a limpet because Saturn will always want to fall back into old, familiar, well-tried, well-worn comfortable habits.

But – and this is a big and important "but" – Saturn **can** be a point of growth. Look at your natal chart to see if there has been a change of Saturn by house and see what you have to learn; the lesson will be found in the house where Saturn is in your natal chart.

An important reminder!

When comparing the changes of the house positions of the ego planets, bear in mind that the position of these planets in the moon node chart is an **illusion** – a mirror image – and that these planets are not there in those houses/areas of life experience and expression **now**. Our task is to learn to function effectively with Sun, Moon and Saturn as they are in the houses in the natal chart. The same applies to the tool planets (☿, ♀, ♂, ♃), and although the impact may not be as strong as it is with the ego planets, it is still worth investigating if a particular planet's change of position has meaning for you.

"What is the significance of a planet which stays in the same house?"

If a planet is in the same house in both the nodal and natal chart, this suggests there is still work to be done in that particular area of the chart – i.e. the house/area of life involved. Perhaps we have to learn a particular lesson again or complete a partly finished task. We can go deeper into the meaning of this house for ourselves, extending our exploration of what its associated area of life expression signifies for us and perfecting our actions there. The planet involved will offer plenty of clues about the nature of the task and what our reactions might be, as well as being an invaluable resource for us to draw upon. It can be used more fully and effectively as it is on familiar territory and has direct access to the unconscious and all that is stored in our personal deep "well" of knowledge and experience.

Examples of Ego Planets Changing Position

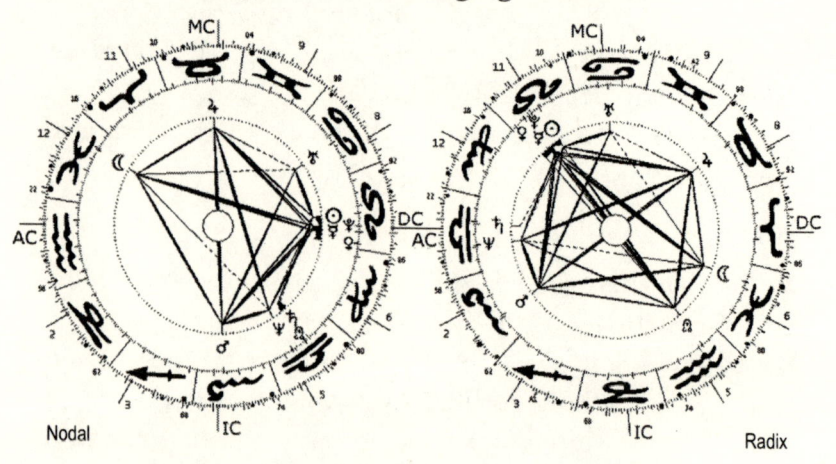

Nodal | IC | IC | Radix

Mike – Moon Node and Natal Charts
08.08.1952, 11:15 (10:15 GMT), 52.36 N, 002.05 W

Mike's moon node and natal charts (above) both have a strong overall aspect structure yet show marked differences in appearance. The Sun in both charts is part of the stellium of four planets. It is in the 7th house in the node chart, but rises to the 11th house in the natal chart. The Moon falls from its position in the 11th house of the node chart to the 6th house in the natal chart, and Saturn rises from the nodal 5th house to the natal 12th house.

Summary: Sun rises, Moon falls, Saturn rises.

The orientation of the small aspect structure in Sally's nodal and natal charts (opposite) is different, and this may be significant in a chart where the aspect structure clings to one hemisphere or quadrant of the chart. Her Sun stays in the same house – the 12th – in the natal chart. There is no movement away from this house, indicating work still to be done in this area of life with this planet. The Moon in the 10th house of the node chart falls to the 2nd house in the natal chart, and Saturn falls from the 11th in the node chart to the 12th in the natal chart.

Summary: Sun stays in the same house, Moon and Saturn fall.

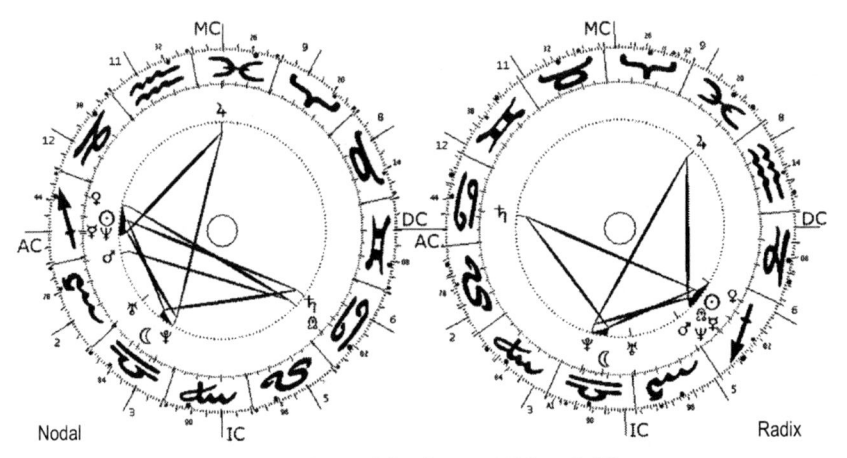

Rachel – Moon Node and Natal Charts
08.12.1974, 20:30 GMT, 05.33 N, 000.13 W

Rachel's distinctive chart appearance (above) stays pretty much the same, although the orientation is different. Uranus remains unaspected and Mars loses its one aspect in the natal chart. Her Sun falls from the 12th house in the node chart to the 5th house in the natal chart. Moon falls slightly from the nodal 2nd house to the natal 3rd house, with Saturn rising more noticeably from the nodal 5th house to the natal 12th house.

Summary: Sun falls, Moon falls, Saturn rises.

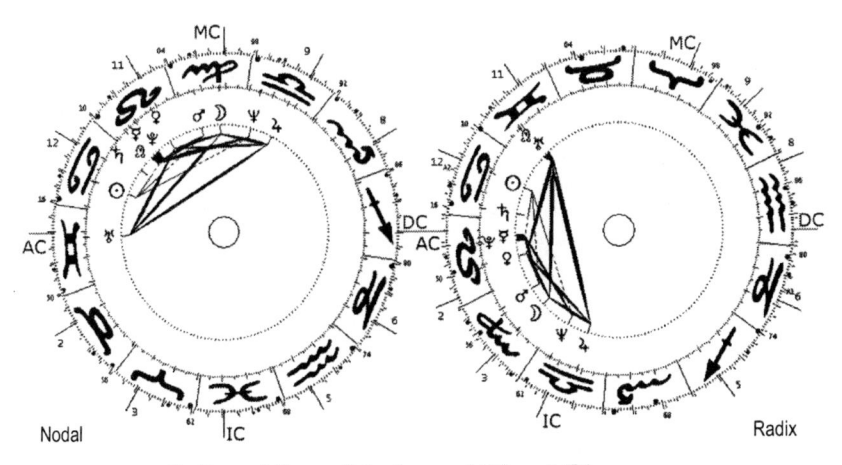

Sally – Moon Node and Natal Charts
04.07.1946, 06:05 (05:05 GMT), 53.25 N, 002.55 W

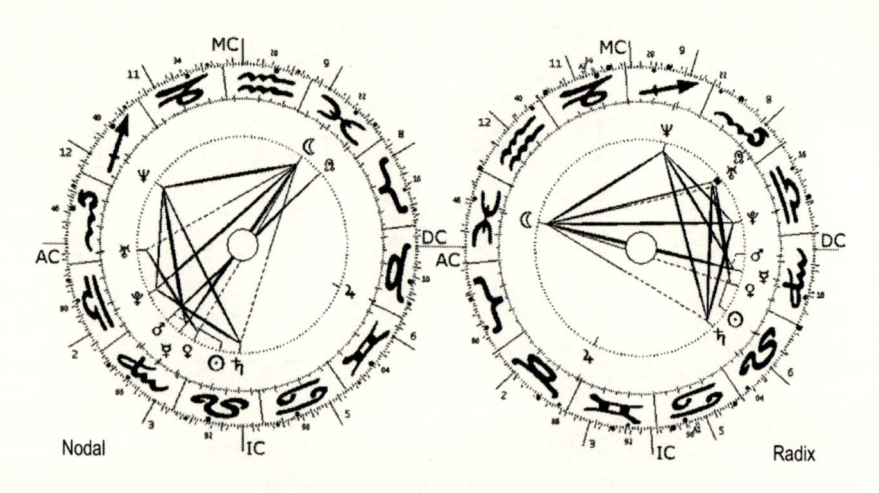

Sarah – Moon Node and Natal Charts
11.08.1976, 21:40 (20:40 GMT), 53.05 N, 002.27 W

Sarah's Moon acts as a tension ruler in both charts, and Jupiter remains unaspected. Her Sun rises from the 3rd house in the node chart to the 6th house in the natal chart. Moon falls from its high position in the 8th house of the node chart to the 12th house in the natal chart, and Saturn rises along with the Sun from the 3rd house in the node chart to the 5th house of the natal chart.

Summary: Sun rises, Moon falls, Saturn rises.

Worked Example

I use my own moon node and natal charts here as an example because I am most familiar with them. I also have Saturn in the same house in both charts.

5. Reconciling Past, Present and Future 125

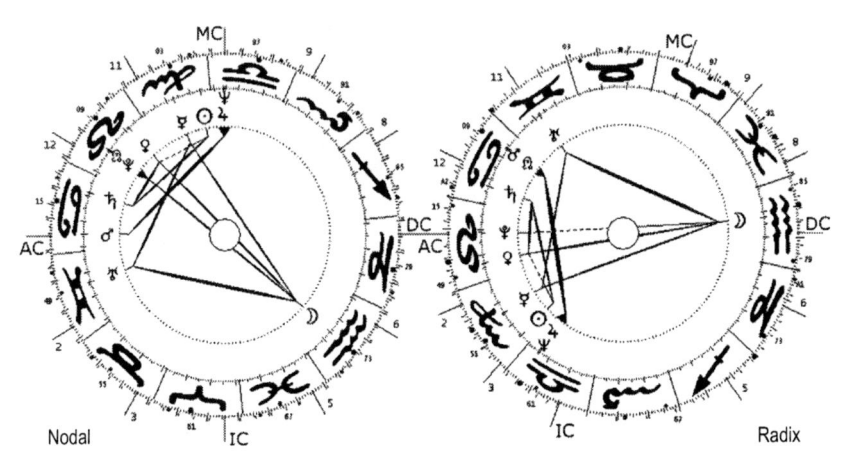

Joyce Hopewell – Moon Node and Natal Charts
19.09.1945, 02:30, Tadcaster, UK

☉ Sun

My Sun is in the 10th house in the node chart – it is right at the top and the highest of the ego planets. This indicates that I could come from a place of expecting others to respect my position of "high authority" and will imagine that just because **I** think I am right, others will automatically do so too! Bearing in mind that it can be all too easy to lapse back into the behaviour of the node chart, it can be relatively easy for me to come from a place of "I do not just think I am right, I **know** I am right!" and to expect the people around me to fall in with my authoritative stance. Of course, what happens is that I can get knocked back pretty sharply by the environment if I come on strong in this way. The lesson here is to learn a bit of humility, because my Sun falls from the top of the node chart to the bottom of the natal chart. Although it is in the 2nd house, it is close enough to the 3rd cusp to be pulled more towards this area of life. I am reminded here of the saying "You teach best what you need to learn;" my task is to take my own awareness and understanding of personal authority, sense of self and self-knowledge and share it – by teaching it – with others.

☽ Moon

Whereas my Sun has fallen to the bottom of the natal chart, my Moon has risen. It is still the tension ruler of the chart but in the node chart it is focussed on the 5th house. My task in this instance is to apply the knowledge and experience I already have of 5th house relationships and bring these up into the realm of the 7th house. The ability and understanding I have gained of being able to relate to a wide range of people, and to understand some of the games people play in the area of relationships in general, are there to be applied in the context of one-to-one relationships and encounters. This is a particularly valuable resource to draw upon when using astrological psychology with individual clients.

♄ Saturn

Here, Saturn is in the same house in both charts. There is no change of position to work with, but there are countless opportunities for me to draw upon the energies of this planet and perfect my own understanding and expression of it. There is still work to be done with Saturn and the 12th house. But rather than this area of life being a "no go" place, especially as described in more conventional and traditional approaches to astrology, for me it is an area of essential solitude. With Saturn there though, it is not necessarily a place of rest because Saturn is about form and structure. In writing this book I need to have self-discipline and to structure my time and the words I use in order to manifest something in tangible form for you to read. In Chapter 3, I said that I had given a lot of study and thought to Saturn and for me that came very easily as I felt able to draw from within on the qualities and energies of this planet.

Exercise – Practical Work on the Moon Node Chart

Any exploration of this chart will be personal and subjective to you, the reader/student. Bearing in mind all the points covered so far, it might be useful now to do this exercise to give yourself a deeper understanding of your node chart and your ego planets. You will need your moon node and natal charts for this exercise, and a pen and notepad. You might like to record this exercise so that you can listen to it, or read it all through first before you begin. Do not worry if you cannot do some of the things in the exercise – it is not a "test" that you have to get "right". Just do as much as you can the best you can. Stay open to all the possibilities and insights that this experience can offer you.

All you need to remember is which house in the moon node chart your Sun, Moon and Saturn are positioned in. Take a look at your node chart now to remind yourself of this, then put the chart aside and settle comfortably into your chair, or on the floor if you prefer. Then allow your body to relax... let any tensions that have built up inside you gradually melt away... and settle into your own quiet space.

Imagine that you are sitting at the centre of a courtyard, and that it is a beautiful day. The sun is warm and you are feeling very comfortable and relaxed in the sunshine. Take a moment or two to really feel yourself sitting in this place, and to get a clear picture of the courtyard. As you sit there, taking in the scene around you, you become aware that there are twelve doors leading off the courtyard. Each of them has a number from 1 to 12 on it, and you notice that some of them also have the symbols of the planets on them. These may be painted on in gold or silver, or in different colours, or they may be represented in other ways.

Now find the door which has the symbol for the Sun, and the number of the house that it is positioned in, and move towards it. Have a good look at the door... what kind of door is it? What is it made of? What colour is it? What is the handle like? And how is the symbol for the Sun

[Exercise continues on next page.]

represented? Then take hold of the handle, open the door and go inside.

Spend some time now exploring this area behind the door marked "Sun", meeting anyone who happens to be there and taking time to fully experience what you find there. Do not censor anything in this experience, and just allow your exploration of what is behind this door to unfold, as it will offer you insights and understanding of the Sun's position in your node chart. If you do not get any definite images or pictures, do not think you have failed! You may receive impressions, colours, and maybe a sense or feeling of the place you are exploring, and all of these are valuable.

When you feel that you have spent enough time exploring this area, turn back towards the door that leads into the courtyard, saying goodbye to anyone you have met there and thanking them for any assistance they have given you. Back in the courtyard, find somewhere to sit and make a few notes for yourself of what you experienced behind the door marked "Sun".

When you have done that, once again relax into the warmth of the sun and take in the scene around you, noticing the twelve doors leading off the courtyard. Now find the door which has the symbol for the Moon, and the number of the house that this planet is in. Get up and go towards the door. Once more, look at it closely. Is it different from the previous one? What colour is it? What is the door like? How does the symbol for the Moon look? Is there a handle? Find a way of opening the door, and go inside.

Spend some time now exploring this area behind the door marked "Moon", meeting anyone who happens to be there and taking time to fully experience whoever or whatever you meet with. Remember, as before, not to censor anything as you encounter what is there. Stay open to what you might discover in this place which can give you insights into the position of the Moon in your node chart.

When you feel that you have spent enough time exploring this area, turn back towards the door that leads into the

[Exercise continues on next page.]

courtyard, saying good bye to anyone you have met there and thanking them for any assistance they have given you. Back in the courtyard, find somewhere to sit and make a few notes for yourself of what you experienced behind the door marked "Moon".

For the final part of the exercise, once again relax into the warmth of the sun when you have completed your notes. Take in the scene around you, noticing those twelve doors which lead off the courtyard. Find the door which has the symbol for Saturn, and the number of the house that this planet is in. Stand up and go towards this door, noting what it looks like and if it is different from the Sun and Moon doors. Take note of its colour and what it is made of, and of how the symbol for Saturn is shown. See if there is a handle. If so, what it is this one like? Open the door and go inside.

Once again, explore the area behind the door marked "Saturn", meeting anyone who happens to be there, and take your time to fully experience whatever is there. Remember not to censor and to stay open to what you might discover here. It will help you understand more about Saturn in your node chart.

When the time feels right to return to the courtyard, bid farewell to anyone you have met behind this door and go back through the door into the warm sunshine. Find somewhere to sit and make some notes for yourself on your experiences. Then when you have done this, allow yourself to relax once more in the warmth of the sun, knowing you have made an important journey and have done some good work along the way. Gradually allow all the images and experiences you've had to fade… move your hands and arms, your neck and shoulders, your ankles and feet… and any part of your body that needs to stretch. Come back fully into the here and now and spend some time considering what you have learned about your ego planets and their positions in your moon node chart.

◻ ◻ ◻ ◻ ◻

Age Progression in the Moon Node Chart

The moon node chart has it's own Life Clock, and by progressing the nodal Age Point, shadow qualities from the node chart can be observed coming to light. Behaviour which has not previously been recognised may emerge along with behaviour patterns which follow well-worn circuits. Habitual responses and reactions may be triggered.

- Age Progression is traced anti-clockwise, as for the natal chart
- Age Progression is measured at 5° per year in each house, so each 30° house = 6 years
- The Age Point conjunct or opposite a planet in the moon node chart will bring shadow qualities and behaviour to light – these will include things that might otherwise be repressed, behaviour that could be habitual. When this happens it could create problems in life; crises may arise when what had formerly been repressed comes into consciousness.

When working with your own moon node and natal charts, and the charts of family and friends as you put into practise what you are learning, it is important to consider Age Progression in both charts. It is often found that a significant Age Progression feature in the natal chart is reflected in the node chart, thus emphasising the whole experience of the person during that life phase. Even if there are no aspects being formed by the Age Point (AP) in either the natal or node chart, it's worth looking at the sign that the Moon Node Age Point (MNAP) is in, as this will indicate the underlying qualities which are seeking to break through and surface. In one person's case, the natal chart AP moving through Aries in the 10th house was not making any aspects to planets, nor was it in the moon node chart. But in the node chart the MNAP was moving through Libra. This individual felt frustrated and thwarted as many of his Aries-type efforts to initiate new ideas and activities seemed to sputter to a halt. When he was shown that the MNAP was travelling through

Libra, it became clear that he needed to use more diplomacy and tact in the way he was presenting his ideas, drawing on the latent skills and attributes of Libra which was the underlying sign in the same place in his moon node chart.

Intersection of the Age Point

The full effects of the Moon Node Age Point are detailed in *Moon Node Astrology* so I will just touch briefly on the basic features. As both the natal and moon node charts have their own Age Point, and the node chart is a reflection of the natal chart, the Age Point on both charts meets and crosses. The meeting and crossing point is known as the intersection of the Age Point and it takes place twice during the complete 72 year circuit of the chart. When the Age Point in the natal chart meets the Age Point in the moon node chart on the **same degree of the same Zodiac Sign**, this is known as the Crossing Point. This can be experienced as an important and sometimes dramatic turning point in life. It's significance may not be recognised at the time, though, and it is usually in retrospect that the period of life that it spans is seen to be influential. As this event happens twice (once every 36 years) our age and level of conscious awareness at the time need to be considered.

The first Crossing Point takes place somewhere between birth and age 36. If we are young when this happens the first time around, it is more likely that the second Crossing Point will have a greater impact. The second crossing happens between 36 and 72 years.

"Can you give an example?"

If the first Crossing Point takes place when the person is 19, the Age Point will be in the 4th house in both charts. The second Crossing Point will be at age 55 – 36 years later – when the Age Point is in the 10th house. Both Crossing Points will take place on the Individuality axis as the 4th and 10th houses are involved.

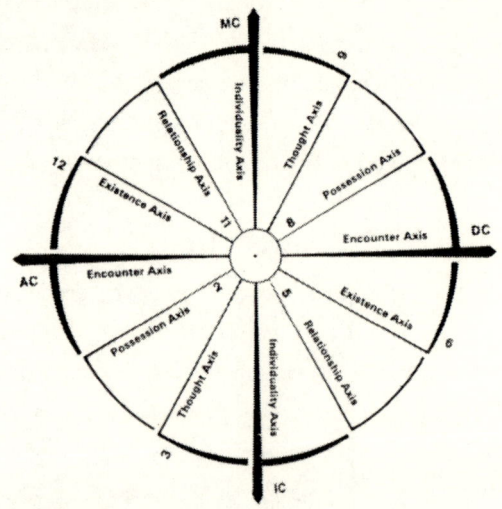

The Axes (See *The Astrological Houses*)

"Is the Crossing Point axis significant?"

Yes it is. It can give useful information about the area of life where challenges will arise, and the nature of the issues which will demand attention and probably some work on our part too. For example, if the Crossing Point falls on the 4/10 Individuality axis we can expect the person to have some problems regarding their own sense of individuality – whether to assert it or whether to sublimate it and bow to the demands and expectations of the collective. If it falls on the 6/12 Existence axis, the person may spend a lifetime working on the theme of this axis, which has a "To be or not to be" quality. They may constantly seek ways to justify their existence, or maybe explore the purpose of their life in order to come closer to some answers to the question "Why am I here?"

"What are the effects of the Crossing Point?"

In general, if life has been fairly quiet and we have been shaped and influenced by the environment before the first Crossing Point, we are more likely to open up and come out of our shell at this time and develop our autonomy and sense of self. If, on the other hand, we have been confident, perhaps even dominant, we are likely to calm down and be rather more passive and much quieter after the Crossing Point.

The first intersection of the Age Points can be striking and, in some cases, more noticeable and significant. If the person changes, grows and develops after the first Crossing Point then the second crossing is barely discernable. However, if the second Crossing Point has a strong, marked effect this suggests that the person learned, grew and developed less than they might have in the years following the first crossing.

Some people describe the first Crossing Point experience as one where sudden drastic, unexpected and dramatic events took place. Big life changes may be involved and we are forced to cope on our own as people or structures around us disappear. However, it is not always as dramatic as that. We may simply undergo a change of orientation in the way we think, or perceive the world we live in. The results of this could be that we extend our awareness into other areas of life beyond ourselves and our own ego and assume more responsibility for the environment we live in and the people we live alongside.

"Do the changes that the Crossing Point can bring happen on the exact day of the crossing?"

No, it does not happen quite as fast as that. The Crossing Point takes place on a particular axis of the natal and moon node chart, which relates to an area of life expression and experience. Changes and a new awareness take place in this area of life over a period of time which covers the months before and after the exact Crossing Point. This can take 18 months to 2 years either side of the exact moment of crossing, so the awareness and change is gradual. It is best to view the Crossing Point as a time of opportunity stretching both before and after the moment when both charts "click" together. This period of time can be likened to the sound of a gong, which starts off quietly, reaches a crescendo and then dies away. In modern urban cities imagine the sound of a police or ambulance siren in the distance, getting louder and louder as it approaches and then dying away as the vehicle moves off into the distance.

Crossing Point Example – Sarah

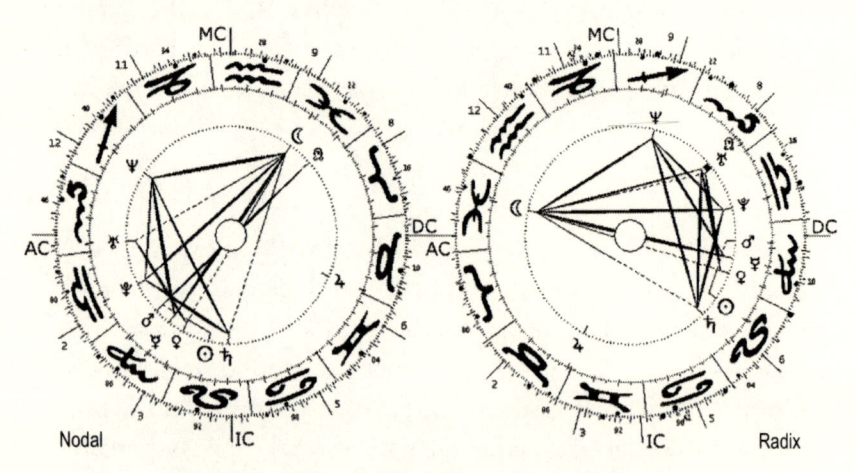

Sarah – Moon Node and Natal Charts
11.08.1976, 21:40 (20:40 GMT), 53.05 N, 02.27 W

Sarah is a professional woman in her early thirties. She works in Education and Training in the National Health Service, and has responsibility for training multidisciplinary staff in Communication Skills and Conflict Resolution.

Sarah was born with a rare genetic condition for which she needs to take medication on a daily basis. There are no outward signs of this condition, but her growing up has included coming to terms with this and accepting it as part of herself and who she is.

I asked her for feedback on her first Crossing Point. Were there were any life events that had been significant for her as she went through this specific psychological life phase – her Crossing Point. The period of time I was looking at was in 1999, around the time she was twenty-two, when the first Crossing Point was taking place on the 4/10 Individuality Axis of both her node and natal charts. I noted that her AP was in the 4th house of her natal chart at this time, and that the period in question spans the Balance Point of the 4th house to the start of the 5th house. Coinciding with this first Crossing Point, her

AP was travelling through the fixed and then the mutable zone of the 4th house, and then on through the stress zone before the 5th cusp.

I explained that the effects of this particular period of life could have extended up to two years either side of age twenty-two, so that although 1999 was definitely a year to consider here, she might also have been aware of significant events from age twenty in 1997, to age twenty-four in 2001. I drew on the aspects her AP was making during this period: a quincunx to Neptune, a trine to Moon, a square to Pluto, a semi-sextile to Sun and a sextile to Mercury and to Mars.

> **Sarah's Age Point Aspects 1997-2001**
> 1998   □♇, ⚻♆, △☽
> 1999   ⚹☿
> 2000
> 2001   ⚻☉, ⚹♂

I asked if Sarah could recall what was going on at this time of her life? Was there anything significant that happened for her, maybe on an inner level? I suggested that there may have been an increased awareness of herself as a feeling, sensing person – maybe she was more in touch with her feelings, more able to express them, articulate them? I wondered if, in 1997, when she was 20 – and onwards during that period – she might have connected more with her ability to stand up for herself and possibly started to realise and understand more about herself and things that fell into the category of "personal growth". Did her ideals come to the fore? Was she getting an inkling of what might be "perfect" and how she might have to change or transform in some way in order to reach any such aspirations of perfection? Sarah says:

> "In 1997 I moved to London to work for a year as part of my degree. I guess I did start to get a greater sense and understanding of personal growth. I attended a two day assertiveness skills course at work in March 1998 which I think was a really positive experience. Lots of people noticed the difference in me and in how I interacted with others. I also started doing a "Praying the Body" course. There were a lot of spiritual/religious people in the group who were open to concepts like healing, energy, the synchronicity between different spiritual approaches. In my final year at University in 1998-99 I felt a lot more at ease and accepting of myself and who I was, of my desires and dreams and I guess this coincided with growing up generally.
>
> I had strong/perfectionist ideals of wanting to do good, contribute, make a difference, and think this manifested in my voluntary work with Oxfam in 2000, handing in a nationwide petition to Downing Street, and going to India to teach. All this happened in 2000 when I was 23/24."

I asked if, during the period in question, and more specifically in 1998, she was aware of a real burst of growing up and moving away from the family environment and establishing herself as an independent person. With the Crossing Point on the 4/10 Individuality axis, it is possible that learning to assert her individuality could be an on-going life theme.

> "I think I really came into my own in 1998 and adjusted to living in London. I started to build a network of friends and live the London scene a bit. Probably being on my own, and away from the safety net of friends I had at University was very good for me as it gave me more independence and confidence in myself as an individual."

I asked if, in or around 2001 at age 24, she started to learn anything significant about herself – perhaps about her ability to assert herself, how she might even "come on strong." Was there a recognition that she has specific talents or skills – was she aware of her ability to communicate well with others, be innovative and creative in her own right?

> *"I probably started to learn something more about myself, and how I can come on strong or be very assertive. I think I also realised in 2001 that I was a very good and efficient worker, both in the temporary job I had and the position I hold now, and that others were impressed with this. I had the opportunity, if I'd wanted it, to become a permanent employee when I was doing the temporary job, and earn a lot of money at it, too. But the opportunity I chose to take was to move into training, which I don't regret as I enjoy my job a lot."*

I asked if, during the period of time in question, Sarah had found she was able to "come out of her shell" more than beforehand. I asked if up until this period of her life, she had felt less confident, less in control of her life, and if perhaps she tended to respond from a place where she felt she was "expected" to behave in a certain way.

> *"I would agree with this. When I was younger I think I developed a concept of how I should behave in order to please and appease people. I think I probably still do this now to some extent, but I'm doing it more from a place of knowledge and wisdom rather than fear, and I have more control over it and can see it for what it is."*

Crossing Point Example – Rachel

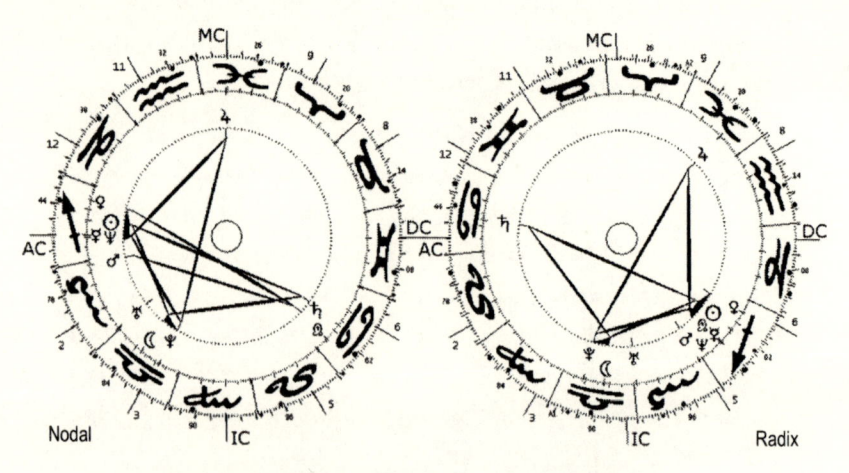

Nodal | IC | IC | Radix

Rachel – Moon Node and Natal Charts
08.12.1974, 20:30 GMT, 05.33 N, 000.13 W

Rachel is also in her early thirties. She is married, has two young children and works in retail.

Rachel comes from a mixed-race background; her mother is half-Ghanaian, half-Lebanese; her father is Lebanese. She was born in Ghana and lived there until the age of 8, when the family moved to Beirut.

I asked her for feedback on her first Crossing Point. Were there were any life events that had been significant for her as she went through this life phase? The period of time I was looking at was in 1988. She was thirteen and the first Crossing Point was taking place on the 3/9 Thinking axis of both her node and natal charts. I noted that her Age Point, in the 3rd house of her natal chart at this time, had just moved into Libra and was in the cardinal zone of this house.

I explained that the effects of this particular period of life could have extended up to two years either side of age thirteen, so that although 1988 was definitely a year to consider, she might also have been aware of significant events from 1986 when she was eleven, to 1990 when she was fifteen. During the time covered by the Crossing Point, her Age Point moved from the cardinal zone to the Balance Point, through the fixed zone and then on to the Low Point of the 3rd house. I noted specifically that during this period, her Age Point made a conjunction with Pluto. I drew on the many aspects her Age Point was making during this period: a square to Venus, a sextile to Mars, a semi-sextile to Uranus, the Pluto conjunction, a sextile to Neptune, a quincunx to Jupiter and sextiles to the Moon's Node and Mercury.

> **Rachel's Age Point Aspects 1986-1990**
>
> 1986 □ ♀
> 1987 ✶ ♂
> 1988 ⚺ ♅
> 1989 ☌ ♇, ✶ ♆, ⚻ ♃, ✶ ☊, ✶ ☿
> 1990

I asked Rachel if she could recall what was going on at this time in her life. Rachel says:

"I was living in the Lebanon and when I was fifteen we emigrated to Germany, where we lived for 2 years. I think this was around the time I was diagnosed with an underactive thyroid and also started wearing glasses."

I asked Rachel if anything of importance and significance happened in her life during this period. I wondered if it might have included issues associated with her feelings, or with growing up, maybe even changes that she felt were thrust upon her in some way, like moving unexpectedly. Or maybe something happened that felt completely out of her control?

"It was around this time that my mother decided to take control of her life. She had been saying to my father for a while that she wanted to leave the Middle East. The war was pretty bad and the racial

harassment was starting to get to her. Dad was not ready to leave; he felt settled so he kept putting her off. Mum took matters into her own hands and with the help of her sister living in Germany, organised our escape from the Lebanon. We secretly packed our bags over a week and kept them hidden from dad. This was awful. I cried so much and I begged her not to make us go. I loved dad and I wanted him to come too, or I wanted to stay. I remember smelling his suits, trying to capture his smell so I would never forget him.

When the day came no-one knew we were going, so I wrote my best friend a long letter telling her how much I was going to miss her. The next part is like something from a movie. Mum and us girls (Rachel has sisters) were at the port waiting to board the ferry across to Cyprus. We had gone through the check-in desk where they had looked at our papers and we were about to board the ferry when dad appeared. My heart burst, I was so happy. Mum was very upset. Dad's eyes were red, something I had never seen before. We all got back in the car and drove home. Mum and dad did a lot of talking. Mum's first question to dad was "How did you know?" Dad said my friend had come to our door in tears asking if we had already left for Germany. Mum never held it against me for writing that letter, and she laughs about it today."

Rachel's family stayed in Beirut for another two years, then they did eventually go Germany. The period of time we are looking at is when she was between eleven and fifteen, the years either side of the Crossing Point, so experiences here could also be significant. Rachel gives more details of what happened at age eleven, when she stepped outside her "security zone" for the first time, and noticed how this made her feel different.

"I was very insecure and extremely shy when I was a child, but at the age of eleven I invited the residents of the apartment block where we lived to my birthday party. Most of them showed up, including my great-grandmother. Up until this moment, no one had ever done this as birthday parties weren't celebrated in this way; they were quiet affairs. Even after this I always felt as if I was outside the box, like

I didn't belong. The Lebanese people, especially my father's family, treated me very differently from my sisters (this was the way it felt to me). I was a different colour and perhaps they were ashamed of that (Rachel is olive-skinned like her mother – she calls herself black – whereas her sisters are lighter-skinned like her father.) I even once heard family members telling my mum that it would be best to take me to Europe to get me married because I wasn't going to find a Lebanese husband due to the colour of my skin. Sweden was apparently where I would find a suitable husband!" (Rachel is married to a white Welshman.)

I asked her if, during 1988 when the Crossing Point was exact and her AP was making the conjunction to Pluto, she went through a period of realising her own true identity. For a teenager that can be hard – perhaps even more so in Rachel's case – because she had to learn to assert herself. Was she able to connect with, or get an inkling of, her own power? I wondered if particularly, between August and November 1989, any new vistas opened up for her and if she maybe got a hint that relationships were an interesting area of life – one that could yield plenty of learning opportunities for her?

"I wasn't a rebellious teenager and I always sought the approval of my elders and peers. We had emigrated to Germany by this time and I was attending the International School in Hamburg. This experience was paramount. I went from a strict religious school in Lebanon to a school that believed the student body was in control of their own destiny. During this time I realised I actually enjoyed school and I went from being introverted and shy to someone who went to the school dance - and danced! I was no longer a wallflower and felt confident in my own body. I knew my strengths and my weaknesses and used what I knew about myself for my own benefit and to help those around me."

Rachel said that she came out of her shell more when the family went to live in Germany, and that at the International School she attended there, she no longer felt she stood out as being "different" because the students came from diverse nationalities.

These brief real-life examples offer a flavour of how differently each individual is likely to experience the intersection of the Age Points in the natal and moon node charts, reminding us that it is important to stay open to what we discover when working with our own and other charts. With what has been covered in this chapter in mind, you are encouraged to explore and research the moon node chart for yourself.

Chapter 6

Following the Spiritual Path

In this chapter we will be looking at how astrological psychology and the use of the natal chart can aid us as we work on our spiritual development. People who begin to wake up and live their lives more consciously often speak of being "on the spiritual path." As this is the subject of this section of the book, now would be a good time for you to clarify for yourself exactly what **you** understand by the term "the spiritual path." What does it mean for you? Does everybody mean approximately the same thing when they use this term? Do we assume that others will automatically understand us if we talk about "the spiritual path"? It is important to pause and consider what this means for us, because it is a relatively easy thing to say yes, we are on the spiritual path. But if we do not have a clear idea for ourselves of what we mean by this in practical terms, we could end up by paying lip service to "being spiritual" and only go through the motions.

"Can you give an example of what it means to be on the spiritual path?"

Being on the spiritual path could mean we are less focussed on material gains and acquisitions. We might have voluntarily given up some of the things in our lives which we took for granted, or are perhaps less interested in those things which previously had been of central importance. We are most likely to have developed a deeper interest in and appreciation of the natural world. We could be working for the common good in some way, maybe meditating regularly, or offering something we can do well or enjoy, as an act of service to others.

> **Exercise – Spiritual Path**
>
> Spend a few moments reflecting on your own understanding of what being on the spiritual path means for you, along with some of the practical ways in which you can ground this and make it manifest in your life. Give some examples of how this works out for you in your everyday life. These examples might relate to very simple things, but they are all important, and most important of all is that you ground your spirituality and make it real in your everyday life. Note them down as you may want to refer to them later.

In this chapter we will be looking at how some specific chart features can point the way towards the spiritual path and help us bring more spiritually oriented qualities into our lives. The application and manifestation of what we discover along the way depends upon how grounded and practical we can be in our expression of spiritual energies. How effectively we can live these out in tangible ways is the key. What we do on the spiritual path has to have true grit and legs, and be able to walk its talk.

We will be looking at the three levels at which the planets function, and considering if we are using them in asleep, waking or awake mode. The importance of the transpersonal planets will be explored, and how we might cooperate with their energies. The Moon's North Node and the nodal axis will be covered as this is often an important signpost showing our next step and way forward, and we will look at the significance of the sign on the ascendant. Included will be a reminder of the importance of the circle at the centre of the chart, and of how this can be used as we follow the spiritual path.

The Levels of the Planets

The effectiveness with which we can use the psychological drives symbolised by the planets in the chart will depend upon the level of conscious awareness with which we are able to use them. If they are functioning at the asleep level, we are unlikely to be fulfilling our potential through them. It makes sense, then, for anyone seeking to develop spiritually to understand how the drives associated with the tool and ego planets (see page 47) can be raised up to higher levels of expression. In order to do this we have to live more consciously to get the very best we can from these planets.

Asleep Level

We need to consider what we mean by "asleep" in the context of a planet functioning, responding and reacting to the environment. What does the "asleep" level suggest to you? In astrological psychology it is the level at which we use our drives in a fundamental and primitive way. They function from the unconscious level where survival instincts dominate, so life is sustained instinctively and impulsively. We may experience intense emotions at this level and will focus on having our basic physical needs met. For the moment, leave aside trying to relate this to any specific planet, and concentrate on ways in which your psychological drives might respond or react in an "asleep" manner. How would you recognise this kind of reaction or behaviour if you saw it in yourself or someone else? At the asleep level, the psychological drive associated with a planet would be expressed in raw, unaware behaviour where pure survival was paramount. The planet's expression would be unsocialised, ego-centred, and society and the rest of the world would not be considered. The planet would be unconscious and asleep and there would be a **"Me"** syndrome in evidence – of no responsibility except to self. Follow up these ideas by making notes on any additional thoughts you have of how asleep behaviour might manifest.

Waking Level

We move on now to what we mean by "waking" in the context of a planet's function. What does "waking" suggest to you? In astrological psychology we would consider the waking level as where we learn to develop self-understanding and become more consciously aware of ourselves. At this level we are more able to direct and control the energies and drives associated with the planets, moving away from using them instinctively and at the level of pure survival. It is at this level that we begin to attain a balance between survival needs and taking charge of our lives. How would you recognise awake behaviour if you observed it in yourself or someone else? Once again, leave aside trying to relate this to any specific planet and just focus on how you would recognise waking responses. Planets at the waking level would either be more consciously aware or moving towards this position. There would be a recognition of the needs of others beyond those of the individual concerned and behaviour would generally be far more socialised and interactive. Evidence that conscious awareness was growing and developing would be observed, such as cooperative behaviour and a willingness to take more responsibility. At the waking level the move is made from **"Me"** to **"Me and You"**. Make some notes on any additional ideas you might have of how a planet might be expressed at the waking level.

Awake Level

Now that we have arrived at the "awake" level you probably have a much clearer picture of where this is heading. How would a planet express itself and its energies and drives at this level? In astrological psychology this is the next stage on from attaining balance and control in our lives. Here we would be fully awake and able to use the will to choose consciously, make our own decisions and act accordingly. There would be an impetus to live a spiritually infused life, being more open to the voice of intuition. How would you recognise or experience this if you were to observe it in action? What does being "awake" suggest to you? A planet functioning at this level would be fully conscious, alert and aware. There would be a distinct lack of the ego needing to be fulfilled through this planet, and instead evidence of altruistic behaviour and actions. The planet would function on the level of giving without any expectation of receiving. It would fully participate in life without the need to impress anyone or gain recognition. There would be a willingness to assume full responsibility for self and actions taken. When planets function at this level it is no longer a matter of **"Me"**, or **"Me and You"**, but of **"Us"**. There is an awareness and a responsibility toward the whole, an inclusiveness. This is not easy to achieve. Can you recognise any of these traits or this kind of behaviour either in yourself or others? If so, note them down.

"Can you give examples of how some of the different levels might be observed in the tool and ego planets?"

Mercury, symbolising our drive to communicate, would at the asleep level be a baby babbling, mimicry, learning by rote (like learning your times tables at school), and incessant talking without listening to the other. Awakening, it would manifest in intellectual arguments and discussions, maybe showing off knowledge or pontificating. Awake, Mercury would be expressed through creative writing and the ability to connect ideas and cross-refer them.

Mars asleep can be observed in road rage, anger and aggression which is quick to flare, and in raw survival behaviour. Awakening, it can be seen in competitiveness, assertiveness and the drive to achieve. When awake, Mars is expressed in courageous behaviour where leadership qualities and a pioneering spirit are in evidence.

Asleep, the Sun could be expressed as stubborn wilfulness. At the waking level, this becomes self-confidence and the ability to use and direct the personal will and exercise good judgement. When fully awake, the Sun manifests in behaviour which is selfless and honourable as the person acts as a willing agent for the greater good.

Saturn asleep might feel like being chained and held down, unable to move. There would be fear of moving beyond known limits and boundaries. At the waking level, Saturn would be cautious and careful, steady and reliable. Boundaries would be tested, security needs met with solid structures and rules in place. At the awake level, Saturn would have less need of such structures and would be more internally secure, able to act as a wise mentor and benefactor who offers guidance to others.

It is important to remember that whichever tool or ego planet is being considered, the chances of us functioning consistently at one of these levels (especially the awake level) is small. We are human, with human faults and failings, and are continually changing between these levels as we go about our daily lives. Whilst we might aspire to express our psychological drives at the awake level all the time, sadly this is not what happens. We move up and down through the different levels, and if we are observant we might catch ourselves operating at the waking or awake level from time to time; if we are operating at the asleep level it is more likely that we only recognise this in retrospect. The key to monitoring our own progress of the levels we are expressing is constant vigilance and honesty with ourselves.

Exercise – Tool and Ego Planets

These practical exercises may help focus attention on the levels at which the tool and ego planets are functioning.

- Choose a tool planet – Mercury, Venus, Mars or Jupiter – and divide a clean sheet of paper into 3 columns headed Asleep, Waking and Awake. Write down under the appropriate column the behaviour and responses you associate with that planet at that level. For example, for Jupiter you might write "gluttony and sensual experiences" in the asleep column, "taking risks" or

[Exercise continues on next page.]

"being optimistic" in the waking column, and "good judgement" and "wisdom" in the awake column.

- Repeat this with an ego planet of your choice. For example, for the Moon you might list "needy" in the asleep column, "sensitive and compassionate" in the waking column, and "unconditional love" in the awake column.

- Again choose a planet to work on (preferably a different one) and describe real life situations or experiences of this planet that you have had of it at the asleep, waking and awake levels. Make some notes for yourself.

- Go around your home and select seven objects, each one representing one of the tool or ego planets. When you have gathered them together in front of you, decide which of the three levels of asleep, waking and awake you would assign to each one.

- Choose any one of the tool or ego planets. Taking into consideration some of the features of this planet in your own chart – for example, the number and the colours of aspects it receives, its position in the chart by sign and house and the aspect pattern it is a part of – make some honest notes for yourself on how it operates in your life right now, and at which level.

- Consider how you might bring a greater awareness of this chosen planet into your everyday life.

- Then decide upon and list the ways in which you can work on this planet/psychological drive to encourage it to be more awake.

- Review your progress at the end of one week, two weeks, and four weeks. Note what changes you've noticed and how this has affected your everyday life.

❏ ❏ ❏ ❏ ❏

In summary, if you are on what you understand as "the spiritual path", your aim would be to raise your tool and ego planets to the highest level you can so that they are functioning at the waking and awake levels rather than being asleep. Using these planets with more consciousness and greater awareness is an integral part of travelling the spiritual path. It is not always easy, but it **is** worthwhile.

The Transpersonal Planets

The transpersonal planets – Uranus, Neptune and Pluto – are often "blamed" and treated as scapegoats in astrology for the upheaval and disruption they can bring to our personal lives. Their energies are sometimes viewed as negative and undesirable because the situations they are associated with on the personal level can be unsettling. Such situations could be anything from losing a job or partner, to moving house and feeling life is confusing, full of hefty challenges and sheer hard work. When life is like this there are usually some important lessons to be learned. These may not be easy to take on board, and we are probably not going to like what is happening in our lives either. It would be all too easy to remain stuck with this viewpoint which is a very "asleep" way of looking at things. If we are genuinely on the spiritual path, there is a tendency to regard experiences associated with the transpersonal planets in a more positive light. If we are able to approach life in "waking" mode, the challenges we encounter do not go away, but they are easier to deal with. This can be helped by an understanding of how the more positive attributes of the transpersonal planets might fit in with our experiences.

Asleep, Waking and Awake

The transpersonal planets when asleep will be used unconsciously. We will react and respond without thought. When they are waking, there is a coming into consciousness. We have a greater awareness and are able to direct the planetary drive and energy consciously through the use of will. At the awake stage, we can use the energy associated with the planet in a more impersonal way, without our ego getting in the way, doing what needs to be done for the greater good.

> ### Exercise – Transpersonal Planets
>
> - Write down one negative and one positive statement for each of the transpersonal planets – Uranus, Neptune and Pluto. Your statements might be based on your own personal experience of the energy of these planets, or on your observations of others or your aspirations towards the higher, more "awake" level of their expression.

Once on the spiritual path, we begin to express more transpersonal planetary energies and qualities in our everyday lives. We aspire to be more loving, accepting, powerful, more inventive and creative. However, it is possible that most of the time, we are unaware of **how** the energy of these planets manifests in our everyday lives as they tend to operate and live through us at an unconscious "asleep" level. Bruno Huber was of the opinion that the transpersonal planets have to be **consciously** developed, otherwise they will live us, rather than us living them.

The three transpersonal planets are associated with the qualities of

- **Love** (Neptune/Mutable qualities)
- **Will** (Pluto/Cardinal qualities)
- **Maintenance and Change** (Uranus/Fixed qualities)

♅	♆	♇	Transpersonal
♄	☽	☉	Personality/Ego
♀	☿ ♃	♂	Tool
Fixed	Mutable	Cardinal	

Types of Planets

Uranus

Uranus is known for representing independence, liberty, originality, sudden disruptive events, sudden insights and the "aha!" experience, as well as electronic wizardry and creative boundary shifting. Its keywords are Maintenance and Change as it seeks the perfect world. It is in the Fixed column of the above diagram, on the next level up from Saturn, so maintaining and preserving are part of its role, but it may go about achieving these by creating a whole lot of upheaval along the way! The drive for Uranus is to seek new inventions which will help to maintain life at a steady state and then to make changes. When this mode of operating begins to get stuck and no longer works satisfactorily, it makes changes so that things are established and maintained at a new level until change is needed again.

The drive associated with Uranus takes us beyond the realm of known security so that a new form of increased security can come into being. Nowadays this often comes via new technologies, currently taking the form of ever-evolving communication technologies as found in computers, mobile phones, televisions, recording devices and cameras. Up-to-the-minute washing machines, dishwashers and cars are all enhanced with improved and increasingly advanced technology, designed to make life easier. Home environments programmed to respond to the touch of a finger on a control console are just a whisper away at the time of writing.

Uranus stirs us up, shakes us and wakes us up. If we look at Uranus from a higher perspective – that of creative intelligence seeking expression – we can see that this planet is often associated with sudden, unexpected breakthroughs in the way we think or perceive. These force their way through and our solid and cosy perspective is changed or disrupted. There is an opening, a crack in the texture of our lives, which allows a shaft of bright inspirational light to break through. Uranus is the instrument we use to pierce the fabric of consciousness and security. It acts like a researcher and is the sharp, penetrating mind, motivated by Saturn towards security. Uranus enables us to go forth and find new ways of doing things to make life more stable.

As Uranus is the first of the **trans**personal planets (= beyond the personal) we have to use what is discovered not just for ourselves, but for the benefit of all. With Uranus the aim is to use creative intelligence for researching into unknown spheres but with an awareness of the pitfalls involved if this is done in an ego-oriented, unconscious and "asleep" way.

Uranus Asleep, Waking and Awake

At the asleep level, Uranus will be focussed on maintaining security through the use of technical systems and safety devices. Its stance will be defensive, wanting to protect and preserve what already exists. This can be seen at work in our global community with the claims of superpowers that they have the right system for universal security. At the waking level, Uranus can be revolutionary, eccentric and able to break down boundaries. People expressing Uranus at this level have a magical allure; they appear to step out of normality and to have access to realms and phenomena that cannot be explained, such as psychological illusionists, hypnotists and those using mind control. Uranus, when fully awake, is a researcher. The search, at this level, is all-important. Knowledge is only temporary and there is no final solution. At the awake level Uranus can access pure creativity and remain open to insights.

"How does Uranus fit in with astrology? Isn't it known as the planet of astrology?"

Uranus is the planet most frequently associated with astrology because it is associated with research and using the mind at a higher, more evolved level to seek out truths and find answers about the causes of what makes things tick. It can take us beyond mundane existence and inspire us to look methodically, systematically and scientifically at the world around us.

Exercise – Astrology and Uranus

- At this point it is worth pausing to ask yourself why you are interested in astrology. Why do you want to become an astrologer? What prompted you to begin your study of astrology? Make a few notes for yourself on your reasons for embarking on this path.

- Write down a Uranian experience you have had and say which level you think it was at. Were you aware of this at the time? And would you be more aware of it now?

Neptune

Experiencing Neptune is often described as being lost in a cloud on a foggy day! It is famed and blamed for states of confusion, uncertainty, escapism and lack of boundaries. Its keyword is Love; it takes us beyond the level of the Moon, where we find personal love, to the level of transpersonal love which is beyond the personal and is all-inclusive. Neptune opens us up to identification with the "You", with the other that is not "I". It brings us to the realisation that what is not me is still me, because I can identify with it – partner, parents, children, pets, a tree, a flower, a mountain, a poverty-stricken down-and-out, a starving child in a third world country.

Neptune is seeking perfect love in all its manifestations. It allows us to step away from the level of mind and the realm of meaning and all our accumulated knowledge so we can reach out towards other human beings with love. As love has no limits and no boundaries, Neptune encourages us to rise above any petty mental barriers so we can accept others simply for who and what they are.

Neptune Asleep, Waking and Awake

Neptune asleep will be concerned with finding "ideal" love, the perfect relationship, so in a partnership the person could easily deceive themselves if the situation is less than perfect as they unconsciously seek to fulfil their need for love. At the waking stage, Neptune will be prone to irrationalities, will have a strong social conscience and may devote energy to helping others. Awake, Neptune can be expressed through inclusiveness, selfless love and empathy with the feelings of other human beings.

Exercise – Neptune

- Bring to mind a time when you felt wholly present in a situation and when you felt touched or moved and were able to identify with it totally. This may have been brief or unexpected, but it is likely to be an experience which is vivid and clear and is etched upon your memory.

- Using either this experience, or another Neptunian experience you may have had, identify at which level Neptune was operating. Were you aware of this at the time? Would you be more aware of it now?

Pluto

Powerful, intense and sometimes cataclysmic experiences which bring about change are associated with Pluto. This is the planet – and the drive within us – which demands a complete overhaul of everything that has gone before, and its keyword is Will. Pluto allows us to plumb our psychological depths. What is no longer of use or value is discarded as we confront what is hidden in the darkest recesses of our own personal cupboard under the stairs and have a "spring clean" in order to advance, ever so slightly, on our path towards perfection. In this context, Pluto could be associated with depth psychology and therapy, as well as personal growth.

Pluto can bring about searing and profound experiences which range through the physical, emotional and mental levels of our being, taking us right through to the transpersonal level. With Pluto, there is no messing. Its qualities of power, of acting as a catalyst for change and for apparently causing devastation are not something we naturally welcome with open arms, yet Pluto can bring things to light which would otherwise have remained stagnant and hidden. Experiences which may be very painful at the time, such as the breakdown of a relationship or the loss of someone dear to us, can in retrospect be viewed as cleansing, transformative turning points in our own journey of personal growth if we are able to accept and cooperate with what is happening rather than rail against it.

How we might experience the energy of Pluto could be likened to a volcano which simmers quietly for long periods of time. When it erupts it has a devastating but dramatically cleansing effect, reshaping what existed before and forcing renewal in us. Pluto takes us beyond the level of the Sun, the personal sense of self, leading us closer to the ideal of the perfect being. We have to hold in mind an image of ourselves as the perfect being and of perfection in all things. As we aspire to this we can draw on the qualities we admire in our own personal heroes and heroines to help us. Working with Pluto energy is not about developing our personal will, but about aspiring to cooperate with a higher Will.

Pluto energy is powerful, so understanding how and where this power can be used and directed by us and through us is important. It can be used with self-interest in order to dominate, wield power and manipulate, or it can be used in a more enlightened manner. If we try to utilise Pluto's energy for personal gain, it won't work. Ultimately, we will be toppled.

Pluto Asleep, Waking and Awake

Pluto asleep will rely on external expressions of transformation such as those expressed through dress, speech and behaviour and there will be idolisation of contemporary icons such as celebrities, pop stars, film stars and footballers. When waking, Pluto will show up in strong personal ambitions and power drives and an urge to achieve and conquer through manipulation. Awake, Pluto's energy works in a quieter and more interior manner as the individual concentrates on personal growth which is aimed at being transformative. An image of the perfect being is held in mind and concentrated upon as inner work takes place.

Exercise – Pluto

- Go back to a time (this could be recent or a while ago) when you experienced a change in life as you had known it up until then. The event might have had its own intensity, so be aware that recalling this period of change could bring up some uncomfortable or sad memories for you. Without dwelling on these, acknowledge their presence as you examine how this event may have changed you, and see if you can identify how it has done this. Make some brief notes for yourself.

- Note down a Plutonic experience you have had and see if you can say at which level you feel Pluto was operating. Were you aware of this at the time? Would you be more aware of it now?

Exercise – Transpersonal Planets in Your Chart

Drawing on everything covered so far in this section, together with your own experiences and understanding of transpersonal planets, choose one transpersonal planet to work with. Make some notes for yourself on the following:

- How do you experience this planet in your life?
- At which of the three levels can you see it might have functioned in the past, or currently functions?
- Do you want to notch it up a level?
- If so, what might life be like at this level? What would this enable you to do more of, or be more like?
- What aspect colours does your chosen planet receive? How might this affect its expression?
- Is your chosen planet part of an aspect pattern? If so, which one, and how does it influence the overall motivation of this pattern?
- Is your chosen planet aspecting an ego planet (Sun, Moon, Saturn)? If so, what effect does this have for you?
- Is your chosen planet on a chart angle (AC, DC, IC, MC), house cusp or Low Point? How do you experience this?
- Which house is your chosen planet in? How do you express it in this area of your life?
- Is your chosen planet currently being activated by the movement of the Age Point around your chart?

You can repeat this exercise as many times as you wish, using all three transpersonal planets. If you return to it at different times, you may notice that your responses change too, which would indicate your increasing awareness of how to work and cooperate with the qualities and energies of the transpersonal planets.

The Nodal Axis and the Moon's Nodes

☊ ☋

Sometimes clients or non-astrologers will point to the glyph of the Moon's North Node in the natal chart and ask "What does that thing like a headset with earphones mean?" This question offers an ideal opportunity for the astrologer to explain the significance of the nodal axis in the context of needing to "tune in and listen" to its message and bring greater awareness of what it indicates into everyday life.

The nodes are not planets and have no energy of their own. They are significant points in the chart and can be used as signposts pointing in two opposite directions. One points to an area of life experience and expression which is well-known and familiar. The other indicates where we could be heading on our own path of personal and spiritual growth. The message of the south node is "stay put, you're safe here." The message of the north node is "move forward and grow, even though it may feel scary."

Physically the nodes are points in space where the Sun's ecliptic (its apparent path around the Earth), and the Moon's ecliptic (its actual path around the Earth), intersect. The glyphs for the north (ascending) ☊ and south (descending) ☋ nodes indicate where these paths intersect. Much has been written about the symbolism of the nodes, which are sometimes called the Dragon's Head (north node) and the Dragon's Tail (south node). The head is advancing and leads the way; the tail follows along behind. There are strong associations here with coming and going, advancing and retreating, making headway into new areas and staying put in the safety of what is already known.

Exercise – The Nodes

- Stop for a moment and consider those areas in your life where you feel you are staying safe or facing new challenges. These might include real life situations where you could be advancing or retreating and staying safe. Make some notes for yourself, perhaps dividing a sheet of paper in half lengthwise and noting your "forward motion" on one side of the paper and your "staying put" activities on the other. What comes out of this short exercise may not immediately relate to the nodal axis in your chart but it is intended as a starting point for looking at where you might be stuck in your life, and where there may be areas of challenge right now.

"What do the nodes mean in the chart?"

The nodes are best thought of as a nodal line, or axis, along which we can travel. Both ends of the line have to be included because the nodes can show us where we have come from. The nodes offer the potential for gaining balance within ourselves and our lives, and they can act as a correcting mechanism when we work cooperatively with them. Through a greater understanding of the nodes we can identify what we already know and have experienced and acquired in the past. We can do this from our stance in the present, where we are now, accepting our current situation together with all the challenges and opportunities it offers. At the same time, we can look towards the future and the direction we can take in order to grow, develop and unfold more fully.

"What does the south node indicate?"

☋ This is like the Dragon's Tail which you can imagine dragging along the ground at the back of the advancing body, led by the head. Its position by sign and house indicates what we come into life already knowing well. This may be

Through the Moon's Nodes we are able to connect with:

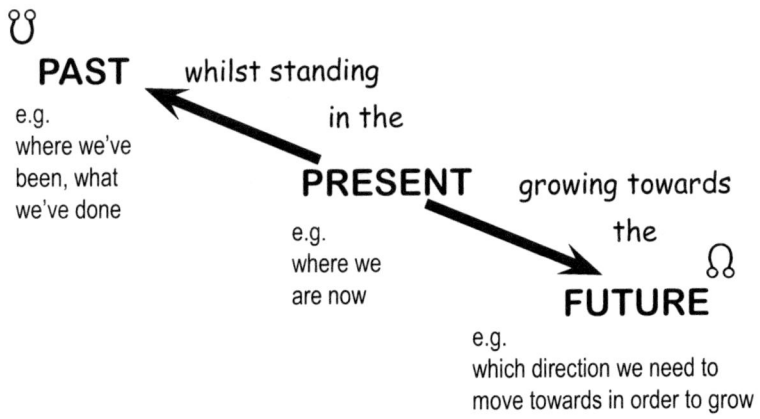

☋ **PAST** whilst standing in the **PRESENT** growing towards the ☊ **FUTURE**

e.g. where we've been, what we've done

e.g. where we are now

e.g. which direction we need to move towards in order to grow

something we bring from a previous existence, or what we are comfortable and familiar with, such our habitual responses, well-known and well-used habit patterns, ways of behaving, relating, responding and being. The south node has a Saturnian quality because it is about safety and familiarity. We may harbour doubts and fears about getting involved in new and challenging activities, and of stepping beyond the boundaries of our well-organised security system. The south node is like a cosy fur-lined rut or an old and comfortable pair of slippers that we're loath to let go of – understandably so.

"What about the north node?"

☊ This is like the Dragon's Head leading the way into new and often uncharted territory. Its position by sign and house gives a clear message of what we can aim for as it shows the direction we can grow towards, if we so choose. The north node has a Jupiterian quality because it offers the opportunity to open up and experience new things. It encourages us to move forward into areas which are less familiar and face the excitement and adventure of rising to new challenges in life. The north node in the chart is like a beacon indicating where and how we can develop ourselves through personal and spiritual growth. Following the direction of the north node may mean turning away from all that is safe, cosy and familiar as we move forward and break new ground.

Using the Huber Method, the north node only is included in the chart and the aspect structure. This is because the north node is considered to be an important feature for personal and spiritual growth, pointing the way forward to our next step along the path. The nodal axis is interpreted first and foremost according to the house axis involved. The houses relate to areas of life experience and expression, and show **where** and which area of life experience we have to grow away from (south node) and move towards (north node). The zodiac signs that the nodes are in can be useful indicators of **how** we behave in these areas, but with the Huber Method it is the house axis where the nodes are placed that is of the greatest significance.

The journey from south to north node may be uncomfortable and difficult, and not, from the point of view of the personality, what we really want to do. There is a saying that often what is good for the personality is bad for the soul, and what is bad for the personality is good for the soul. As with all personal growth work, it is not a bad idea to retain a sense of humour as you travel the spiritual path!

The Nodal Axes and their Tasks

The 1/7 Axis of Encounter

The nodes in the 1st and 7th houses span the I/You Encounter axis which is where we meet the world, and the world meets us. This is a cardinal axis, with action and contact taking place across it. We focus on ourselves in the 1st house, and encounter others in the 7th. Interactions in the 7th house can bring learning and greater awareness of ourselves over in the 1st house; we can look into the mirror provided by the 'You' and if we are aware and willing to act, we can make changes and adjustments to ourselves, the 'I'.

"How do the nodes work on the 1/7 axis?"

With north node in the 1st house and south node in the 7th, we are able to relate to others easily, more often than not putting their needs above our own. We may even define ourselves through others and need to be needed in order to establish our own sense of self. In our encounters with others we will feel guilty if we do not put the wishes and requirements of those around us first. Because of this, we could easily overlook taking proper care of ourselves. The task here is to develop the other end of this axis, and rather than fall into the comfort zone we are familiar with in the 7th house, to redress the balance by giving attention to 1st house matters. This means learning to develop a stronger style of presentation of self, daring to put ourselves and our own needs before the needs of others, and working consciously on any feelings of self-doubt we may have. We could choose to develop more self-reliance and independence and be more aware of ourselves as having an identity separate from the needs and demands of others.

When the north node is in the 7th house and the south node in the 1st, the position is reversed. A person with a 1st house south node is likely to have a strong and well developed sense of self. They will be independent, will not rely on others and will consider their own needs first. They are more concerned with self than with the "You" and will be reluctant to commit formally to one to one partnerships. Getting married or forming a binding legal relationship could prove difficult for them. Their task in the 7th house is to focus on developing the other end of the axis by making contact with others and recognising that their needs exist too. Whilst it will be far more comfortable for them to remain isolated and independent, their mission is to relinquish some of their independence and throw their lot in with a partner, offering to share and co-exist rather than keep themselves to themselves. Learning how to do this will probably be challenging and uncomfortable, as will putting self second and others first, but doing so helps to redress the imbalance, and offers huge benefits in the area of interpersonal relationships.

The 2/8 Axis of Possessions

This is a fixed axis, where the motivation is to hang on tightly to what is already there. The nodes span the 2nd and 8th houses, where possessions of all kinds feature. In the 2nd house on the "I" side of the chart, those possessions are "mine" – and what is mine makes me feel safe and secure. These do not have to be material possessions, although sometimes they most certainly are; personal characteristics, skills or qualities which support our sense of self-worth can be considered as something we possess. In the 8th house we find the possessions of the "You" – the belongings of other people, the belongings of society at large, together with the requirement that we pay our contribution towards them. The possessions of the 8th house might include street lighting, the emptying of our rubbish bins and local public facilities, all of which are paid for in taxes. These are often managed by large institutions, some of which we might feel powerless against because of their size and the law's insistence that we contribute towards them and their upkeep. This is a fixed axis, making it challenging to work with, as the strongest impulse is to preserve and maintain what is ours.

"How do the nodes work on the 2/8 axis?"

If the north node is in the 2nd house and the south node in the 8th, there will be a heavy reliance on the structures created by society. There may be an attitude of "things come to me easily" and an expectation that even if life goes drastically wrong, help from outside will be provided, be it by the state, or social services, or by supportive family and friends. Possessions may provide a source of security and will be hung on to at all costs. Money may come from outside sources, in the form of inheritance; the individual may not need to use their own talents and skills to survive. Values, viewpoints, attitudes and belief systems may also come from others and provide a comfortable and easy route to conforming with social mores. The task in developing the other end of this axis is for the person to establish within themselves a stronger sense of their own self-worth. This can be done by examining their own personal values and honestly appraising these alongside the values which they have taken on board from their surroundings. Developing innate talents, skills and abilities is an important way forward and the person can then begin to bring out and use the potential they already have within themselves rather than rely on what others can give them.

With the north node in the 8th house the person will probably already have possessions and belongings which they value, together with a strong sense of self-worth. There may be a dislike of the structures of society, such as laws, the requirement to pay taxes and authority establishments and organisations like the police or military. The urge to hang on to what we already have and own is powerful, yet the task is to learn how to live by these laws and accept them as a necessary part of society. Big strides forward can be made if we undertake new ventures which include giving back something to the society we live in. Maybe we can draw on some of the material goods or wealth, or even the talents we have, and put them to good use to benefit society as a whole.

The 3/9 Thought Axis

This mutable axis involves all kinds of thinking and learning, and being mutable and flexible, changes can take place here. Old structures and forms, especially thought systems and outmoded routines, can be broken down as new ones are created. There is a focus on the ideas and thinking of the collective in the 3rd house, with greater emphasis on more specialised, refined and "higher" ideas in the 9th. Whereas what is thought about and talked about in the 3rd house might be shared gossip, news of celebrities and their lives and local news, what would provide stimulation in the 9th house might include deeper, wider ranging topics like global matters and international news.

"How do the nodes work on the 3/9 axis?"

With the north node in the 3rd house and the south node in the 9th we are likely to be more comfortable with matters of higher mind. We could be interested in philosophy, or on a quest for wisdom and understanding, so books, study, reading and discussion with others of like mind could be our passion. In fact, we may be a bit of an intellectual snob and think we know it all! We might look down on collective thought patterns, unable to understand or connect with what interests people on a collective level. Perhaps we feel our knowledge is superior to common knowledge. This will give our approach to life an "ivory tower" feel as we struggle to relate to how others think and see things; we will be far more comfortable being aloof and separate. Our task, then, is to come on down from that ivory tower and connect with what the collective is buzzing with interest about. It may feel very strange, even threatening to do this, but it is the way forward. We have to open up to collective knowledge, pick up some of the current buzz words and jargon, and immerse ourselves in life in the general community rather than in the rarefied one we are more familiar with. We also have to cultivate humility as we do this, acknowledging that ordinary people have ideas of value too. Then we can begin communicate with the collective and develop the common touch.

When the north node is in the 9th and the south node in the 3rd, this is reversed. With a 3rd house south node we can already relate closely to collective thought forms and knowledge and we will feel reassured by this. It will be as easy as relaxing in an undemanding pair of jogging trousers. We will look up to professors and other so-called learned people and revere their opinions, supposing that they must be right as they have knowledge and wisdom. Our strengths lie in the ability to be practical and deal with facts rather than explore underlying concepts. The task for us lies in cultivating our capacity to think for ourselves. We must learn how to voice our own ideas and to not be afraid of speaking out. This can be difficult since we will probably have to break away from established norms and expectations to do so, so courage is required. Our thinking has to become lateral and divergent, taking us away from more conventional and convergent approaches. This is not easy as it challenges the status quo of the collective.

The 4/10 Individuality Axis

This is a cardinal axis, where initiatory action and movement towards asserting our own individuality takes place. We learn how to stand on our own two feet and lay claim to our own sense of self on this axis. In the 4th house we may cling to the security of all that is familiar, where we are accepted and nurtured by the collective as long as we conform and fit in. The 10th house is where we have to shine, gain recognition and express our authority out in the world and at the highest point in the chart.

"How do the nodes work on the 4/10 axis?"

If we have the north node in the 4th house and the south node in the 10th, we are already quite familiar with being in a position of power or authority. We may be a leader of some kind. Perhaps we are the chair of an organisation, have a managerial position at work or are successful in what we do so that we stand out in some way. We are accustomed to being noticed, to asserting ourselves as an individual in our own right. Because of this, we could easily think we are superior to others, a cut above the rest, and we will seek to hold on to this position for all we are worth. We may have come far in life, perhaps from humble beginnings, so it could be preferable to conveniently forget our family and origins as we strive to maintain our high profile position. Our task is to develop some humility and get down from the "high horse" position. This, in some cases, might require a big step down. If we are able to move along the nodal axis to the 4th house to connect with our roots and family, and the place we came from, we will enter into relationships which involve feelings. We could have been living in our heads up in the 10th house; now it is time to redress the balance and engage once again with our roots and family, acknowledging that without the base this gave us to grow from, we would never have reached the position we attained.

With the north node in the 10th house and the south node in the 4th, this is reversed. Staying safe in the comfortable domestic nest provided by home, family and neighbourhood in the 4th house is very alluring, but it is not the way forward. We have become accustomed to feeling protected and nurtured, and in turn we have been contented to allow the expectations of family and surroundings to define our goals. We will be strongly attached to our roots and reluctant to leave our home patch. Our task, then, is to take courage and stand up for ourselves. We have to find our own way and goals in life and pursue our own independence, and this includes breaking away from the safety of the nest. In doing so, we have to detach ourselves from the expectations of the family. We may feel isolated as we pursue this path towards our own individuality because the family and the collective will resist any changes we are trying to make. Following the path of individuality requires determination and courage; if this is undertaken with genuine love towards our family and acknowledgement of all they have given us, the journey is easier as both ends of this axis can be included as a balance is sought.

The 5/11 Relationship Axis

On this fixed axis, change may not happen quickly, there being a natural tendency to hold on to matters related to relationships in general. Once a relationship is established, it can be difficult to confront issues concerning behaviour patterns which have become ingrained. In addition, relationships provide us with a strong sense of security and stability; having them provides one of our basic needs in life and allows us to make close physical and mental contact with others. The 5th house in the collective "You" area of the chart is the arena for physical relationships; in the 11th on the "I" side of the chart we meet on a more mental level of shared ideals, goals and aims.

"How do the nodes work on the 5/11 axis?"

With a 5th house north node and an 11th house south node we are pretty choosy about the kind of friends we mix and mingle with. We enjoy meeting people who are "different" in some way because they are interesting and mentally stimulating for us. We feel more akin to those whose values mirror our own so we tend to be selective about who we spend time with. We might mix with others of the same social status or standing, but ultimately we will gravitate towards people with whom we feel on the same wavelength mentally. We will be concerned with high ideals and forward-looking viewpoints so we will connect with chosen friends and associates on a mental level, and physical aspects of relationship will be played down. The task for the 5th house north node is to learn how to relate in a more down-to-earth manner, moving away from mind and the mental activity of the 11th towards relationships which involve physical touch and real human contact. We have to experiment with relating on the physical level. Leaving aside our comfort zone of meeting on the level of the mind, we can learn how to make contact through touch and body contact. This can be as simple as learning how to give someone a hug rather than standing back formally when the situation and relationship calls for more. The task and the challenge is to experiment with life – real, tangible human life – and stop being aloof.

When the north node is in the 11th house, and the south node in the 5th, we are already familiar with relating to others in a hands-on way. We do not shy away from physical contact and we understand, through first hand experience, many of the games and manoeuvres played out within the context of relationships. We get along easily with others from all walks of life, and gain a sense of security from our many contacts. Our task is to move towards developing relationships with people whose values we share and whose ideals we aspire to. Rather than remain open to all comers, we have to become selective about the people we spend time with. We can become more choosy and discriminating about who we have as our friends, and if we can draw on the experiences gained at the south node end of this axis, in the 5th house, we can take this understanding with us to the "higher" and more refined atmosphere of the 11th house to share with those we meet there.

The 6/12 Existence Axis

We've come full circle and now return to the I/You axis of the chart. On this mutable axis we question our very existence. Why are we here? What is the purpose of our life? What are we meant to be doing with it and what can we contribute to the greater whole? What happens when the going gets tough? Do we roll up our sleeves and face the challenge or withdraw because it's all a bit too much for us? In the 6th house, we confront the "You" and are on the front line of working in some kind of service capacity for others; in the 12th house, we can withdraw deep into the "I" side of the chart away from the hurly burly of everyday life. This can be especially attractive when mundane reality becomes too uncomfortable.

"How do the nodes work on the 6/12 axis?"

With the north node in the 6th house and the south node in the 12th, we may indeed want to escape the practicalities of life by turning our back on them and hanging a sign saying "Do not disturb" on the door. For us, it will be easier to retreat and cease contact with the outside world than face up to the washing up, painting and decorating and tidying the garage. Escape appeals, and we will find ways to remain on the "I" side of the chart if we possibly can. We will opt out, and may even get ill as a means of avoidance. As the pull towards the spiritual dimension is strong, we might even consider joining a religious order, which would offer a structured escapist lifestyle. Less extreme would be go on regular retreats where the details and practicalities of the world can be left behind for a while. The task here is to step away from the inner sanctum of the 12th house and move towards the 6th house where we will meet up with the "You".

Here we will learn how to face the realities of life and realise that we have a duty and a calling to serve humanity in the best way we are able and suited to. We will gain an understanding of how we can give service to others by being there to help and support them. If we are able to go about this cheerfully and with good will, we open ourselves up to receiving the gift of unexpected joy which will come to us from those for whom we work and serve.

If the north node is in the 12th house and the south node in the 6th, we already know a lot about helping and serving others. We probably define ourselves and our life's work through what we do for them, and sometimes wonder how they would manage if we were not there. We are always busily involved in service of some kind, be it fundraising for a charity, helping out at community events or supporting a less able friend or family member. We have a strong sense of responsibility for the welfare of others and readily take on caring duties to justify our existence. The task here is to transfer our attention to the 12th house and the "I" side of the chart. We have to learn how to stand back from the world, and resist the impulse to rush in and sort things out. It is not easy to accept that the world can manage without us, nor that we can exist without the practical involvement which has previously defined our lives. But we have to slow down and withdraw to a quiet place. This may be a physical space that we create for ourselves somewhere in our environment, or it could be our own inner space. Here we have to nurture, nourish and care for ourselves. We might meditate, read, think, listen to music. Whatever we do, its purpose will be to experience guilt-free quality time for ourselves, so that we can emerge once again into the world with batteries recharged, and full of energy to offer what we can where it's needed.

The nodal axes can be likened to a balance or set of scales which can be weighted down on one side, as if the weighing pan is filled to the brim with all things which are safe and familiar. The weighing pan on the other side will be empty and completely ignored, as if it does not exist. We ignore this to our own detriment because to do so would be like closing the door to a room which is full of treasures and valuable things which are there to help us develop both personally and spiritually.

Working with the North Node

When working with the nodal axis, it is useful to note the aspect pattern the node is involved in. Experience suggests that the node can act as a "dumb note" within an aspect pattern if the individual is not consciously working on matters related to the area of life where the node is positioned. Once the north node is activated, the aspect pattern and its associated behaviour and potential take on a new depth and function more fully.

"Is it always the north node that has to be developed ?"

Although the north node usually points to an area of the chart which corresponds to the area of life to be developed, there can be variations. The chart shaping, orientation of the aspect structure and overall picture of the whole chart can mean that the individual could identify more with the north rather than the south node. In this instance, they will live more comfortably in the north node, and ignore the area that can be developed in order to create the necessary balance in life – in this case the south node.

In Roger's chart (opposite page) the focus is entirely on the "You" side, with an emphasis on the 2nd quadrant. The north node is in the 7th house on the Encounter axis. All matters relating to the "You", interactions with others and the needs of people in the immediate "You" environment are paramount, and in the subject's life there is no particular interest or inclination to engage with the self or matters connected with the self.

The nodal axis, as we know, is a balancing mechanism in the chart, and we can use it to bring real balance into our lives. Even if we shy away from the north node, it will always be there. We

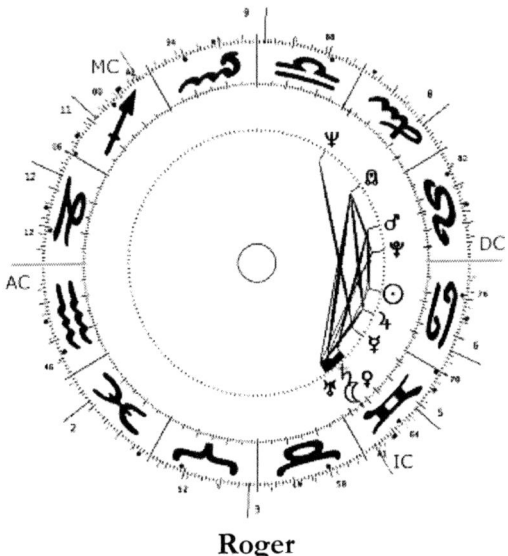

Roger
09.07.1942, 23:00, Lincoln, UK

can choose to ignore it, close the door on it and decide to live exclusively in the south node, but this would limit our growth and journey on the spiritual path. What we can do is acknowledge and include **both** ends of the axis, and be vigilant and aware of which end we are living in. We can do so consciously by making a willing choice to accept that both options are there – the easy, familiar aspects of life **and** the less familiar, more challenging parts too. By doing this we can begin to integrate and synthesise both north and south nodes, but from a central position in the middle of the axis. This, symbolically, can be the circle at the centre of the chart, that clear space which represents both our personal and transpersonal sense of self. We can also bear in mind that the nodes act like a signpost pointing in two different directions, and that each direction has something to offer. The south node – our safe, familiar zone of being – will always be there. But having embarked on our journey towards the north node, our perception of the south node and our desire to be there may change or diminish as we become more aware of the possibilities and potential of the north node.

Exercise – Nodal Axis

Spend some time now making a few notes, or drawing if you prefer, on how you plan to bring some of north node qualities, as indicated in your chart, into your daily life. Be specific and practical. What can you do to ground and make manifest what you have discovered about your nodal axis in the context of your chart? Perhaps you are going to write a letter, make a phone call, express your creativity in some way, do something or go somewhere new and unfamiliar. Whatever it is, it needs to be practical and within the bounds of your capabilities right now. And it also needs to be something which expresses, for you, the qualities of the north node which you are aiming to develop.

The Next Step

Building on the notes/drawings you have made for yourself, make a statement of intent to develop or carry out **one** action in following your spiritual path, using your nodal axis. Decide what this is going to be, making your action or task **simple and easy to achieve.** Be practical and realistic because what you chose will be easier to attain if it is within your range of achievement.

- Say **what** you will do (this can be as big or small as you like but it must fall within the range of practical possibilities)
- Say **when** you will do it (again, be realistic)
- Say **where** you will do it (set the scene, make it real in your own life)
- Say **how** you will do it (keep it simple and manageable)
- Say **who** will witness that you've done this (will someone see or hear you? Will you tell someone? You could even arrange to phone or email someone to tell them.)

Sun Sign, Ascendant Sign

The Sun is an important part of the chart and the personality and can be likened to the conductor of our own orchestra of planets. Its job is to be in charge, leading and directing, so it is important, if we want to use the Sun as effectively as possible, to understand as much as we can about it and what it symbolises for us if we are travelling the spiritual path and are seeking a deeper engagement with life. The same applies to the Ascendant, or Rising Sign. This sign and its qualities are often described as the mask or persona we assume and project when we meet with the external world, but the sign on the ascendant has specific significance when we are seeking to develop spiritually as it can take us beyond the ego level of the Sun. Esoterically the ascendant sign indicates the qualities we should strive to move towards, acquire and express when on the spiritual path. Having an accurate time of birth is essential as it will give the correct ascendant sign.

The Sun, the Sense of Self and the Will ☉

The Sun is a cardinal planet expressing cardinal energy. It embodies the drive to assert and create, and it is important that this part of us is developed and strengthened so that it can be expressed clearly and without fear. It should not be hidden away like a bright torch under a damp blanket, but allowed to shine and be seen.

What does the symbol for the Sun – a circle with a dot in the centre – suggest to you? How do you see this, and how would you describe it to someone who didn't know any astrology? For example, you might say that it symbolises a sense of "I-ness", a sense of self, and refer to the circle, known as the circle of spirit, with its central point of focus representing that "I-ness". The Sun is representative of a sense of self, but what does that mean to you? How would you describe your own sense of self?

Make a few notes for yourself using the questions posed as your starting point.

The Sun is the sense of self we gain through the use of the mind and our own decision-making processes. It is connected with the ability to willingly take full responsibility for ourselves and not blame others when things go wrong. Linked with the Sun is the use of the will – the **strong will** which gives us determination and the capacity to keep going, the **skilful will** which endows us with sound common sense and the ability to be flexible and adaptive as we work towards our goals, and the **good will** which enables us to include others and to work selflessly for their benefit as well as our own. With the Sun we gain a sense of self awareness through the mind as we express go-ahead, initiatory, active energies. The Sun makes us goal-oriented, with energy following thought, leading to the formation and manifestation of ideas. The Sun demands that we use our creative potential, which contributes to our uniqueness and individuality. All these traits can be developed and encouraged to help us strengthen the Sun and gain a greater, more centred self-confidence. We should aim to be devoid of ego needs or the urge to prove that we are "the greatest". On the spiritual path, this attitude is redundant.

"How can I work on developing my Sun?"

If you have been working through the practical exercises in this book in sequence, you will remember that the Sun has already been touched upon in an earlier chapter, so you may wish to refer back to the notes you made then to refresh your memory. Then try out the following exercise.

Exercise - Developing Sun Qualities

Divide a clean sheet of paper in half and write "Positive" on one side, and "Negative" on the other. Then make a list of the positive and negative traits you are aware of and which you associate with your own Sun Sign. Include your own personal likes and dislikes about this sign. Now isolate **three positive traits** which you want to develop and strengthen. Make brief notes for yourself on how practical and achievable this might be, and how you think you might do this. If you decide that what you want to achieve is not feasible for you right now, put it on a "future" list rather than discard it. You can always return to it.

Take time with this exploration and relate your findings to real life situations and your own life experience. Decide (using your Sun of course!) which of the three positive traits you have identified you will work on developing and strengthening first, and carry this awareness into your everyday life, putting your decision into practise and making it become a reality.

The Ascendant Sign

If your time of birth is accurate you will know that the Ascendant Sign in your chart is the correct one; if your time of birth is uncertain there will be some doubt about its validity. However, much can be gained through understanding the principles involved, and even if you are not able to work reliably on your own ascendant sign you will still be able to learn how an understanding of the significance of this sign can be helpful when travelling the spiritual path.

Are there any planets conjunct the ascendant? If so, these will strengthen, help and intensify the qualities of the sign. They will also be helpful in offering you more understanding of this sign, especially if a personal planet is involved. For example, in my own chart I have Pluto conjunct my Leo ascendant, and Venus – a personal planet – is also in this sign.

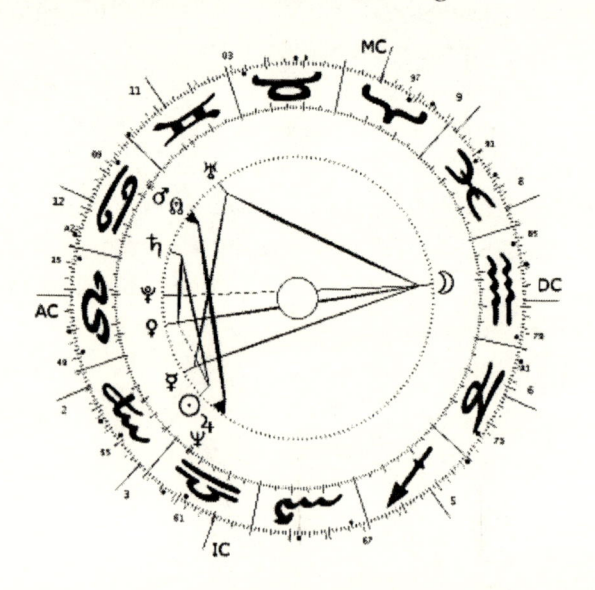

Pluto conjunct the ascendant certainly does have the effect of intensifying the qualities of Leo, but as it is a transpersonal planet it took some time for me to be aware of how Pluto operates in this position. A transpersonal planet on the ascendant can be used unconsciously and at the asleep level, sometimes getting the native into tricky or challenging situations which they are unaware of creating. Once the nature of the planet is understood and there is an awareness of how it might behave in this position, it gets easier and more comfortable to live with a transpersonal planet on the ascendant, especially when there is an understanding of the asleep, waking and awake levels of the planets. With Pluto, I have to remember that the power is not my own and to keep my ego out of the way. Venus as a personal planet in my Leo ascendant sign, on the other hand, constantly offers opportunities for me to experience and learn about relating to others, especially as it is aspected to the Moon close to the descendant.

"What happens if the Sun is in the same sign as the ascendant?"

If this is the case then there is a "double whammy" effect, as the Sun will be expressing the ego personality through the same sign, which might lessen the ability of the individual to grow spiritually through acquiring the traits and qualities of the ascendant sign. Bruno Huber spoke of this situation as one which could weaken the effect of this sign, so it is something to be aware of if you have this in your own chart.

Esoteric Seed Thoughts for the Signs

Each of the signs has an associated seed thought, tabulated overleaf (see *Reflections & Meditations on the Signs of the Zodiac*.) Many students find it helpful to carry with them and meditate on the seed thought for their ascendant sign, since this can offer new and unexpected insights (which don't always make sense on a "logical" level) in their own spiritual work and practice.

Seed Thoughts of the Signs of the Zodiac

Aries	I come forth and from the plane of mind I rule
Taurus	I see, and when the Eye is opened, all is illumined
Gemini	I recognise my other Self and in the waning of that Self I grow and glow
Cancer	I build a lighted house and therein dwell
Leo	I am That and That am I
Virgo	I am the Mother and the Child, I God, I matter am
Libra	I choose the way that leads between the two great lines of force
Scorpio	Warrior am I, and from the battle I emerge triumphant
Sagittarius	I see the goal. I reach the goal and see another
Capricorn	Lost am I in light supernal, yet on that light I turn my back
Aquarius	Water of life am I, poured forth for thirsty men
Pisces	I leave the Father's Home and turning back I save

Exercise – Ascendant Seed Thought

How do you react to your own ascendant sign's seed thought? Does it have meaning for you, or relevance to your life? Does it inspire you and offer you something to grow towards? Make some notes about your initial reactions to your ascendant seed thought, return to them and add to them as this thought takes root within you and you have time to ponder on it.

Exercise – Guided Journey

To complete this chapter on following the spiritual path, you might like to do this guided journey, based on your own ascendant seed thought.

Make sure you know the words of your seed thought. Sit comfortably and quietly and allow any tensions that have built up in your body to relax and melt away. Still your mind and your many other thoughts and just allow your seed thought to be present. What does this thought mean for you? Allow an image, or a scene in your mind's eye, or any words that come to you to be uppermost in your inner space. Maybe something is happening in your life right now which is associated with the seed thought... Or maybe you just have a strong sense of how the essence of this seed thought might be expressed in your life... Perhaps you have an idea of how things could be if you were to start acting upon it. If you can, relate your impressions to something real in your life, something that has meaning for you. Allow a little time now to develop this connection in any way you want... Spend some time exploring this quietly through the thoughts, images and ideas that arise......

When you are ready, make some notes and/or drawings to express what emerged for you in this quiet reflective meditation, and choose how you might bring what you have discovered into reality.

Finally, recall the importance and significance of the circle at the centre of the chart which was introduced in Chapter 1. This clear space in the chart symbolises a clear and uncluttered centre within you, me, all of us, which we often forget is there waiting to be accessed whenever we need to temporarily step back from the rush of everyday life and connect with the calm pool of energy we carry within us. It can be an invaluable resource as you follow your own spiritual path.

Chapter 7

Working with the Three Charts

In this final chapter we look at how, by using the natal, moon node and house charts together, we can gain a rounded, in-depth and three-dimensional perspective on ourselves. Working in this way allows us, as students of astrological psychology, to understand where we are coming from, where we might be right now in our lives, and how we can move ahead. Using all three charts together we can choose to develop those aspects of ourselves which have come to light during the study of our own charts. We can choose to move forward and grow beyond any limitations imposed upon us by our upbringing, which are no longer appropriate.

Worked examples of the charts of two real people are included in this chapter. The first example is of someone who knows a little astrology, but who has had several astrological counselling sessions and is positively focussed on her own personal growth and development. The second example is of someone who has studied astrological psychology and the Huber Method for herself. Both subjects have given feedback; that of the second subject uses astrological terminology relevant to the Huber Method.

Several of the techniques outlined in this book are referred to and all three charts are used. For students trained in the Huber Method of astrological psychology, it is always strongly recommended that they draw on what the three charts, used together, can offer when working with clients. In the latter stages of the training courses offered by API(UK), students gain practical experience of working in this way on their own charts and the charts of others. I hope that all readers will gain some additional insights into how to work with the three charts in this final chapter of the book, drawing on the examples here and the feedback given.

Example 1 – Claire

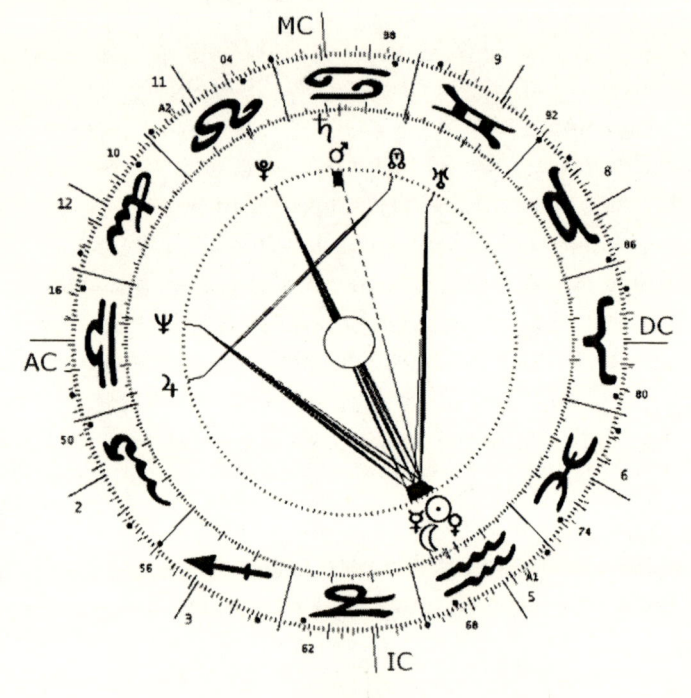

Claire
1.2.1946, 22:45, Kettlewell, UK

Claire is a recently retired woman in her early sixties, whose appearance and vitality belie her age. She worked professionally in teaching and careers guidance, is newly remarried, having been widowed in her early fifties, has two grown-up sons and is a grandmother. She has had several astrological counselling sessions, and agreed to offer feedback on this overview, in which all three of her charts have been used.

Hers is a striking chart. Completely linear, it offers several images: a firework shooting out a spectacular display, powerful searchlights scanning the skies, arms raised heavenwards and an as-yet-incomplete set of lines trying to form a complete recognisable shape. On first seeing her chart, Claire said it reminded her of a conical flask, as would be used in a laboratory. Staying with the idea of a shape trying to be complete in order to be recognisable led me to speculate on a possible inner drive to control the shape her life takes on, as she has Mars/Saturn on the MC. Pluto also sits in a dominant position at the top of the chart, providing a focal point for the opposition aspects to the planets positioned at the bottom.

Her inner, unconscious motivation is restless, searching and initiatory, fuelled by the cardinal quality of the linear aspects. The aspect structure moves in a vertical direction, indicating a strong pull towards individuality, yet it is firmly rooted at the bottom of the chart by the stellium of four planets in the 4th house. Any upward movement and aspiration towards individuality will stem from her having a firm and secure base. With Sun and Moon involved in this stellium, both heart and mind will have to be engaged in any action she might take in this direction. Claire says:

"I certainly identify with these statements. I have tended to feel anxious when faced with situations which I cannot control, and, whilst areas such as thinking, learning, mental exploration, are very important to me, I seem to need a firm secure base – I see this as roots, grounding me – in order to have the confidence to try new things."

The ratio of colour in the chart is not particularly well balanced. With 3 red : 1 green : 6 blue aspects it lacks in green aspects which bring awareness and the ability to view things from a third pole, so there could be a tendency to approach life from an "either/or" perspective. She could help offset seeing things in a mainly black-and-white way by consciously bringing greater awareness and questioning to all experiences and life situations she encounters. Hers is a chart lacking in a cohesive "togetherness" of its component inner parts. It is tangential, potentially scattered and unconnected, but the 4th house stellium offers a firm rooting influence, and visually most things appear to start and end here. The stellium, therefore, seems of considerable importance. Although both upper and lower hemispheres of the chart are equally occupied by planets, the emphasis, once again, focusses on the 4th house. The I/You sides of the chart also appear equally balanced, but if just the personal planets are considered, the "You" side is more heavily weighted with the stellium sitting firmly in the 2nd quadrant. A focus of planets in this quadrant indicates an ability to adapt, to please, fit into the surroundings and assume the expected behaviour and mores of the surrounding environment. This reflects and supports the initial speculation made on the chart image and a possible unconscious drive to control the shape of her life.

> *"Yes, I can make judgements in 'black and white' terms and I am aware of my tendency to 'want to please' or to 'go along with' what others want."*

As there are no complete aspect figures in the chart, only lines, it is worth referring briefly to the moon node and house charts at this point (opposite page.)

Here we can see that both charts have complete aspect patterns. The node chart contains a Large Talent triangle and a direct Dominant Learning triangle. The house chart, likewise, has a Dominant Learning triangle, a single Ambivalence figure and an almost-complete Search figure. This suggests that Claire can draw upon the inner mutable motivation that both these charts offer to help her "get her act together", i.e. to assist her if she is seeking to pull her life into shape and be more focussed. It is also worth noting that Jupiter, unaspected in the node chart, is in a separate trine aspect to the north node in her natal chart.

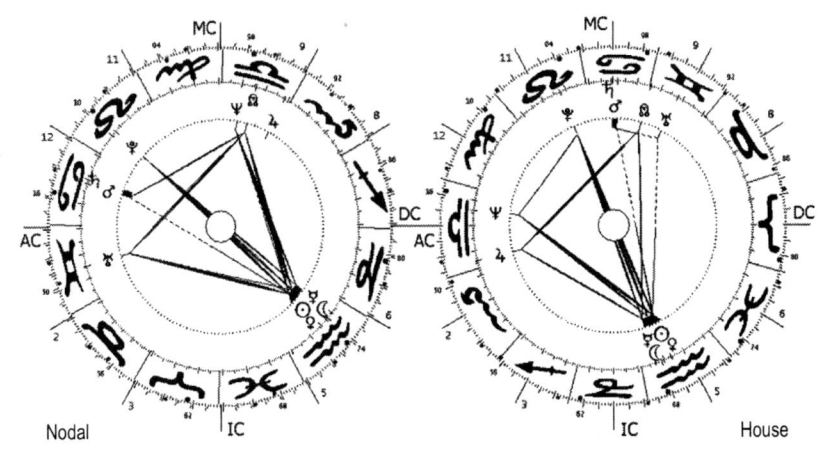

Claire's Moon Node and House Charts

This raises the possibility that her most important lessons in life, especially those relating to herself (as Jupiter is in the 1st house in her natal chart) will come from her own experiences. We will return to these two charts later. Having discovered that they both have complete aspect patterns, and that the house chart has more green aspects, which could be a very useful resource for her, we will now look further into Claire's natal chart.

Considering the placement of planets in the Dynamic Energy Curve of the houses, none of them are placed on a Balance or Low Point, but it is worth noting that Mercury and Moon straddle the 4th house Low Point. Mercury is more pessimistically placed just before it, making me wonder if she might at some stage of her life have doubted her mental capacity to learn, or have felt thwarted when her communications were not always understood. Her Moon is placed just after the Low Point, suggesting a more optimistic and positive approach where feelings and emotional needs are concerned. Perhaps she was encouraged to express her inner child. As both these planets are part of the stellium, their expression will be influenced and modified by the other planets in the stellium – possibly dominated by the Sun in its strong-by-sign position at 12½° degrees. In spite of its low position in the chart, Claire's Sun is still likely to be a powerful force to be reckoned with.

Mars is a stress planet, clearly falling into the stress zone as it is 3 degrees from the MC. In a conjunction with Saturn which straddles this major cusp, Mars could combine its own assertive drives and energies with the stability and staying power of Saturn to form what could be an authoritatively formidable combination at the highest point of the chart. Stressed Mars in this vertical chart will seek to draw on the energy of the Sun, especially when it comes to self-assertion, individuality and the quest for recognition and success out in the world. However, Saturn will keep the energies of Mars in check, ensuring that its assertive behaviour does not go over the top, and could be helpful in organising and structuring Mars' energy. Saturn could also work negatively as a block and dampener against the forcefulness of Mars, making her more wary of asserting herself when she might want to act in this way. Mars in Cancer can be adept at approaching potential conflict obliquely; Saturn could collude in this by reining in the energy and drive of Mars.

The Family Model in Claire's chart shows Sun and Moon (father and child) bound closely together in the 4th house stellium alongside Mercury and Venus, with Saturn (mother) on the other side of the chart as the highest of the Family Model planets.

My speculation on her childhood experiences of her parents is that she was very close to her father and that their relationship was harmonious. I would expect they had plenty to talk about, and that the focus of their interactions and activity would be the home, because Sun and Moon are together in the 4th house. I would also be curious to know, because both planets are in Aquarius, if Claire's father had introduced her to scientific ideas, or ways of thinking, or if he was a forward-looking man with humanitarian ideals.

> *"Up to the age of 11, when I went away to boarding school, I felt incredibly close to my father, and yes, he was passionate about mathematics and biology (the interest in science has travelled down the generations to my son!)"*

Her relationship with her mother I would hypothesise as being different. The close bond of the conjunction that Moon has with Sun is missing in this relationship as Moon and Saturn are linked by a one-way quincunx to Mars, which is conjunct Saturn. This suggests that the bond here between child and mother is less immediate and direct. It has to go via Mars, so there may have been some aggravation between them, and as a green aspect is involved there could have been times when Claire felt uncertain about her relationship with her mother. The connection could have been worked at, however, as a long-term project which would eventually have brought them closer in later years.

Claire was very close to her father and describes her relationship with him as loving and joyful, with many interests and activities shared in the home and family setting. What did he encourage as she was growing up?

"My dad was a talented, mainly self taught, violinist. I was encouraged to learn the violin as well and, although it has given me much pleasure, I have never felt confident that I was as good as other people felt I should be. As I became older, my relationship with my dad became much more difficult – we clashed a lot and I began to feel that I could never meet his expectations of me."

Her mother, as Claire describes her, was kind but firm, and not quite the epitome of Mars/Saturn, as might be expected at first glance. Did she rule and dominate the household, which was her domain, giving credence to the high position Saturn in the chart?

"I don't recognise this description of my mum. I remember her as being dominated by my father (and possibly me!) I became much closer to her in later life, in particular when I had children of my own."

As always, recollections of Family Model experiences are subjective, and as astrological psychologists and counsellors we can speculate and hypothesise about how someone might have experienced their own family and upbringing, but we always have to be receptive to what each individual's experience of this was.

To summarise so far:

- Claire's chart images have a "spectacular" flavour which begs attention: the firework, the searchlights, arms raised heavenwards in a gesture of epiphany, effort required to complete something not yet quite complete
- Linear/cardinal motivation, indicating restless activity; scattered aspects with a lack of coherence; no complete aspect figures in the natal chart, but these present in both node and house charts
- Vertical direction indicating she is motivated to be noticed, gain recognition of some kind, stand out as an individual in her own right
- Lack of green aspects in colour ratio; predominantly red/blue
- Lower hemisphere emphasis with leaning towards "You" side; strongly tenanted 2nd quadrant
- No Balance Point planets; Moon and Mercury close to Low Point; stressed Mars; Saturn strongly positioned in 10th house; both Sun and Venus strong by sign at 12 degrees
- Sun and Moon in stellium of 4th house planets in Aquarius; Saturn conjunct Mars on MC
- Possible close and binding relationship between Claire and her father; more ambivalent relationship with her mother.

Nodal   Radix

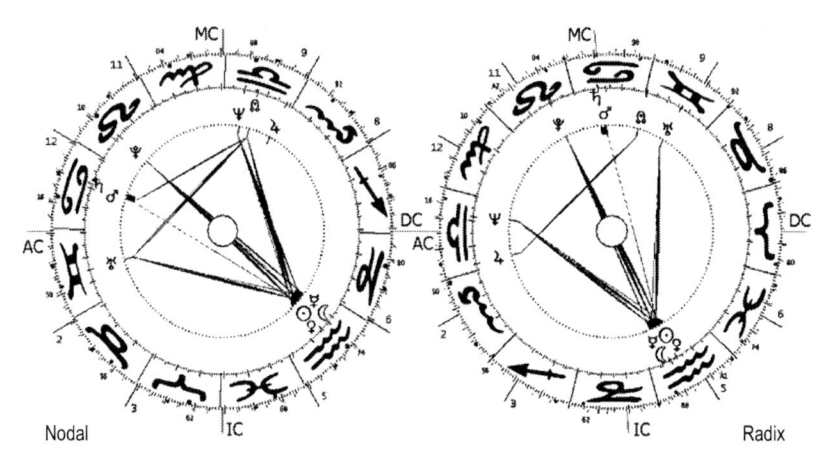

Claire's Moon Node and Natal Charts

Claire's node chart viewed alongside her natal chart offers additional insights into what she can draw upon to help her as she grows in awareness and takes on some of the challenges her natal chart presents. We also have to remember that she may find it easier to relate to and express what her node chart shows.

This chart is dynamic in shape and contains a completed Large Talent triangle and a direct Dominant Learning triangle. What might she be naturally good at, or talented with? What can she do that does not need much working at? The Large Talent triangle is pinned by planets and the north node, all in air signs – are ideas and thinking central to her talent? Jupiter is unaspected in this chart; could she sometimes find it too risky to move forward, do new things and be adventurous? Does unaspected Jupiter in the node chart encourage her to ignore and neglect such Jupiterian things as perceptive sound judgment and what she learns from experience, as Jupiter is connected to the north node in her natal chart by a lazy linear trine?

> *"I have always seen this as an innate lack of courage – I think I can see what to do in certain circumstances but sometimes am afraid to put myself 'on the line'."*

Both Sun and Moon, in the 5th house in the node chart have fallen slightly to their 4th house placement in the natal chart. This suggests that Claire's task is to take her experience, knowledge and authoritative understanding of the way people behave and relate to one another into the realm of the family and immediate neighbourhood. Through her Moon, she may already know how to get her emotional needs met in the hands-on arena of the 5th house; her task is to apply this experience to the family scene and seek satisfaction there. Saturn has risen from the 12th house in the node chart to be at the very top of the natal chart, strongly positioned in the 10th house just after the MC. This indicates that Claire is able to bring her own private observations and her personal inner, and possibly unexpressed knowledge and understanding to bear on the area related to career and individuality. It is interesting, at this point, to note the possible significance here of her work as a careers advisor, a job she retrained for later in life.

"This is, perhaps the area of my life where I feel most comfortable. I feel incredibly lucky to have had a career which, I feel, used what skills and talents I have."

We turn now to Claire's house chart to look at how her upbringing and conditioning could have enriched or diminished her as she was growing up.

Viewing both charts together (next page), there are clear differences. Her parents and those who influenced her in her early years expected something different from what is shown in the natal chart. The house chart offers a contrasting picture, with several complete aspect figures and more green aspects. The colour ratio changes from 3 red : 1 green : 6 blue in her natal chart to 4 red : 3 green : 5 blue in the house chart. Claire gains red and green aspects, enhancing her ability to actively use her energy and be sensitively aware; she loses some of the more passive blue. The greater share of green aspects in this chart makes it better attuned to helpful, conscious growth.

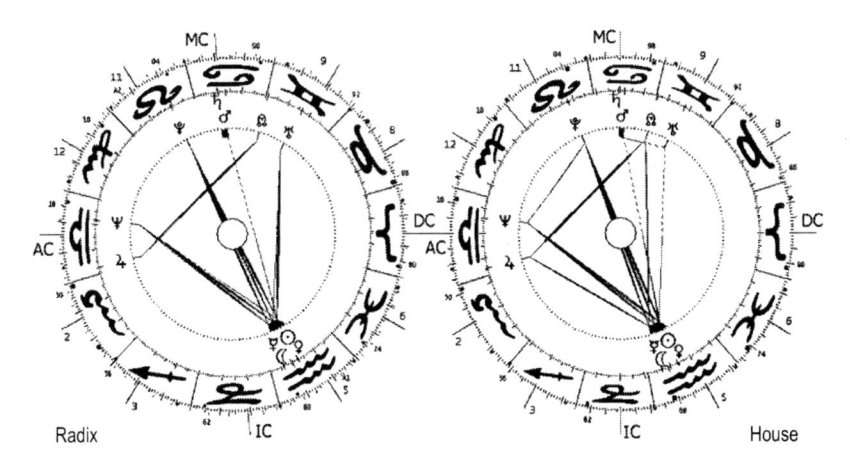

Claire's Natal and House Charts

"I like the sound of this!"

The shaping/motivation in the house chart is dynamic, consisting of triangular mutable figures, suggesting that she was encouraged to be more flexible and adaptable, and less tangential. This could help offset the restless impatience of the linear natal chart's inner motivation. The house chart offers the potential to learn and complete lessons and shows less focus on having to make things fit together in a recognisable shape. It is enriching, offering support and structure for the fragmented, linear natal chart and indicates that her conditioning and the messages she received as a child were beneficial. The Dominant Learning triangle pulls the isolated Jupiter and north node in the natal chart into a cohesive learning pattern in the house chart; Mercury is also involved in this figure, hinting at a more rounded and complete approach to learning for her to draw upon. The Family Model also looks more cohesive, with Sun, Moon and Saturn linked, but indirectly, via the not-quite-complete Search figure.

	Total	Crosses - Motivation			Elements - Temperament			
		Car	Fix	Mut	Fire	Earth	Air	Water
Signs	112	44	58	10	9	0	79	24
House	139	78	32	29	63	33	3	40
Diff.	27	34	-26	19	54	33	-76	16

Claire's Dynamic Calculations

Following on from the house chart, a brief appraisal of the Dynamic Calculations can add further depth and dimension to Claire's conditioning, although nothing should be regarded as a "given", and it should always be discussed with the individual concerned to hear how they experience each chart feature that is explored.

Claire's Dynamic Calculations show an overall stress score of +27. This is not regarded as high, but is edging towards the possibility of some pressure when excessive expectations are laid upon her by the environment. This reflects the heavily tenanted 2nd quadrant of her chart, where she is likely to adapt her behaviour to please and fit in with the collective.

"As mentioned before, this does ring true."

The highest plus scores are found under Cardinal (+34) and Fire (+54) so it would be worth investigating whether her experience is to feel uncomfortably pressurised when she has to take action or be initiatory. Here the demands from the environment are likely to be greater than she has the innate capacity to cope with, and she could end up feeling drained.

"Yes, definitely – however, I also feel I put myself under pressure by exacting very high standards of myself which does leave me physically and emotionally drained."

Claire has equally high minus scores in the Fixed (-26) and Air (-76) columns. Her fixed motivation and airy temperament may be thwarted or unacknowledged in their expression, leading to feelings of inner frustration. A minus score of 76 is very high, so high that the individual could just as easily switch off and stop trying altogether. Yet in Air, this score represents a virtually untapped ability to think, read, research, communicate, teach, learn and study. Claire is aware of this and it is something she has been able to tap into and develop for herself. This is reflected in her professional life as a teacher and her retraining in careers guidance. Currently, she is studying Social Sciences with the Open University and is enjoying this immensely.

"I am loving learning new things."

Claire's Age Point is currently in the 11th house, in Leo. It is close to the Balance Point, and within the next year will move into Virgo. At age 62 (the time of writing), her Age Point is making two sextile aspects to Jupiter trine the North Node, focussing on this separate linear aspect which has been mentioned before, and forming a complete pattern – a Small Talent triangle.

This in itself is significant as it means she is currently connecting with the potential of her 1st house Jupiter and at the

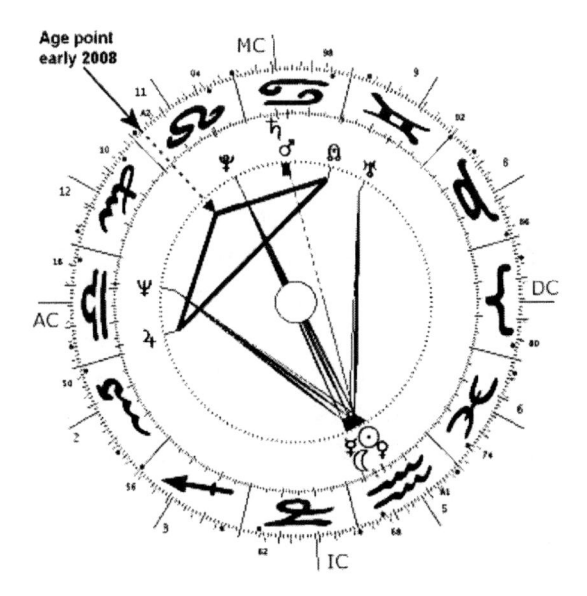

Claire's Natal Chart
The Age Point position in early 2008 is highlighted, forming a Talent triangle through sextiles to Jupiter and Moon Node

same time can seize the opportunity to develop her 9th house node. Claire speaks with passion about the Social Sciences course she is studying; it has clearly fired her interest on a deep level, and in particular she mentions her love of the social history she is learning. Here I speculate once again on the significance of her stellium in the 5th house of her node chart which has now fallen to the 4th house in her natal chart. Social history offers many insights into how people have lived alongside how they live now. She may well be tapping into something she intuitively knows and understands; she could be on familiar ground.

Of additional interest is the crossing of the Age Point in Claire's natal and node charts. The crossing takes place on the 5/11 axis of Relationships. This implies that relationship issues could be an ongoing source of learning for her throughout life, and it may be that this arena is the one where the greatest challenges take place. The first crossing of the Age Points happened in 1971, when Claire was 25 and the Age Point was in the 5th house. At the exact time of the crossing, no other planets were aspected, but the effects of the crossing point can be felt for up to two years either side of the event itself. Two years previously, her Age Point had made direct contact with the planets in the 4th house stellium, and two years later the Age Point changed from an Air to Water sign. Claire recently experienced the second crossing point in the 11th house, at age 61. The second time of crossing can be a time of consolidation. The problems and challenges presented at the first crossing will hopefully have been resolved as the individual has learned and gained more awareness from their own life experience in the intervening 36 years. Whereas the first crossing point took place in the 5th house, when there was less discrimination in the friends that were made and relationships formed, in the 11th house there is more discernment and selectivity at work. Friends chosen here have either stood the test of time or have something significant in common.

Let us speculate now on the role the north node could play in Claire's life as an indicator for possible ways forward. It would be too easy and wrong to automatically assume that Claire is on a spiritual path and simply take it from there. As a client, she could end up feeling bewildered, misunderstood, unheard or plain annoyed if this assumption was made without the astrological counsellor finding out where she was coming from, so it is vital to remember this when practising on the charts of friends and family. Just because you consider yourself to be on the spiritual path, it does not follow that everyone else is!

Because of what she has done in her life up to now, it is unlikely that Claire has ignored the potential of her 9th house node, although she may have had reservations about her ability to develop in this direction. Whether or not she experiences this as part of her spiritual growth would have to first be ascertained, but as the node can be used for both personal and spiritual growth, some careful questioning is usually needed to clarify which.

A 9th house node can stretch us up into the realms of the higher mind. It will want to move away from the mundane because it calls for meatier and more interesting topics of discussion, in-depth study and an exploration of the very meaning of life. These things can be nibbled on in the 3rd house in a superficial way; in the 9th they are meant to be chewed slowly and digested at leisure. Claire's task will be move away from skating over mundane matters in the 3rd house, where collective views prevail, and make a deliberate choice to engage with deeper and more underlying issues. One manifestation of this is her current passion for university-level study. However, the importance of all she has learned and can continue to draw upon in the 3rd house should not be laid aside, as being able to connect with both ends of the 3/9 axis is an important factor in both personal and spiritual growth.

> *"Really all I can say here is that at this stage of my life, I feel more confident, perhaps more aware, certainly very happy and fulfilled. I hope and think that I am continuing to grow and part of this is in some way a spiritual journey."*

Assuming she is on the spiritual path (and this can only be ascertained by talking with her), it could be useful to include a brief mention of the seed thought for her ascendant sign. With Sun, Moon and two other planets in Aquarius, and the Large Talent triangle in her node chart pinned by planets in air signs, she already has an affinity with this element. Maybe it's not surprising, then, that her AC is in Libra whose seed thought is *"I choose the way that leads between the two great lines of force."* Bearing in mind that the significance of the seed thought does not necessarily work at a logical level, it would be worth sharing this with Claire to see if she responds to this and recognises how it relates to her own life.

"I'm still thinking about what this means to me!"

Example 2 – Clara

Clara is a professional career woman in her mid-forties. She works in the public sector, currently in the field of healthcare, and lives with her partner and their two children. She is the main wage-earner in the family. Clara has studied astrological psychology, so is able to comment on her three charts in some depth.

An image that immediately stands out in Clara's chart (facing page) is the large arrow which spans the chart from "I" to "You" side with Moon/Mars at its tip. The arrow is made up entirely of red aspects so this will definitely be an active arrow! It appears to be almost deliberately, perhaps even provocatively, pointed towards the heavily tenanted "You" side of the chart, and greets all-comers to the 7th house of Encounter with two potentially volatile planets in fiery Leo. First impressions are that Clara is not someone to be ignored. It is worth noting that the arrow appears to cut through any distractions as it cuts through the less initiatory blue green aspects. Clara says:

"The first chart image I had was of a crossbow with an arrow (pointing to Moon/Mars) pulled back (by Saturn) to the point of

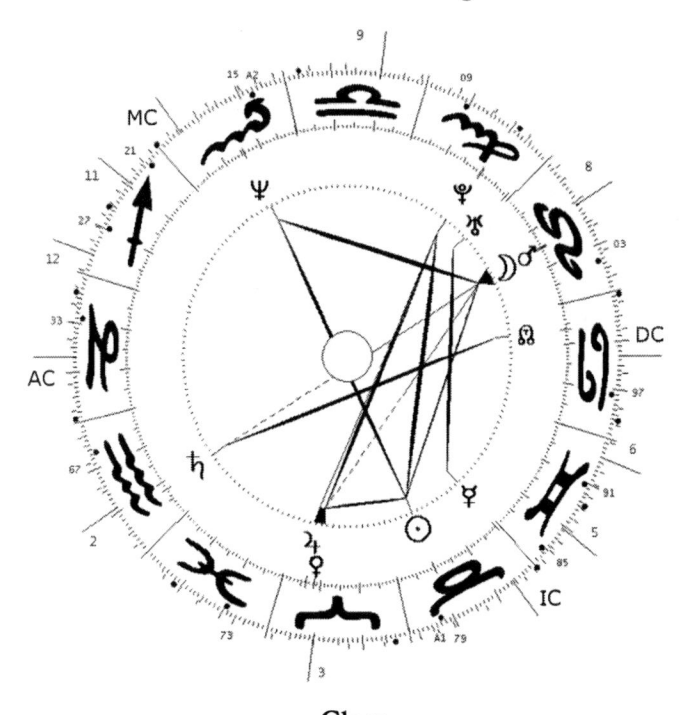

Clara
1.5.1963, 01:55, Louth, UK

greatest tension, ready to shoot out into the environment through the 7th house. Whilst the image could be seen as quite an aggressive or assertive one it's always felt to me more of a defensive posture, being constantly at the ready to defend myself in what I perceive to be a dangerous world. Equally it's given me a sense of being able to look after myself, being armed for the struggle."

Her inner, unconscious motivation is a mixture of flexibility and restlessness; she can adapt and adjust to life changes but she will also get itchy feet, need space and seek to break new ground.

"My mutable shaping allows me to shift and search for answers and adapt to the world around me, learning from my experience. The linear aspects provide energy and enthusiasm for the searching."

The direction of the aspect structure is predominantly vertical, indicating an urge to assert herself and be recognised as an individual of some status, yet there is a distinct pull across the chart by her "red arrow" towards the horizontal realm of interacting with people, perhaps working with them in some way. The arrow is a recognised aspect pattern – the Efficiency/Performance triangle – which includes the highest planet in the chart, Neptune. This suggests she could have high ideals to aim for, and it is possible that she will not want to make compromises on these as her Sun/sense of self is in opposition. Both Sun and Neptune hold in store the energy which fuels Moon/Mars at the apex of this triangle, the arrow's tip. They are stressed before the 8th house cusp so will draw on the energy of the other planets they aspect. Saturn in opposition here acts as a steadying influence, helping her to take aim and conserve the energy that can be released until it is needed.

"As I've begun taking more responsibility for my life I've come to realise that what I need to do is grow up the middle of my chart, rather than focus on the I-side or the you-side. The vertical shaping of my chart means that I need to grow upwards, towards self realisation."

Her ratio of colour is not particularly well-balanced; 4 red, 3 green and 2 blue give a lack of blue and an excess of red which is always readily available to fuel the arrow. Lacking blue, she may find it difficult to switch off and relax, being more driven to work and take action.

"Yes, my chart is very short of blue. This reinforces the crossbow image of being sensitive to the world around me and ready for action."

The chart as a whole has good coherence; a large number of planets are linked into the overall aspect structure. The exception is the separate linear square aspect between Mercury and Uranus, hinting that she may be outspoken, have innovative ideas and is not afraid to go out on a limb.

"When I was about 14 I had an English teacher who on one of my reports simply wrote 'talented but erratic' – which I think about sums up that square aspect!"

Clara's chart has two other aspect patterns – a Search figure and a Small Learning triangle. These are connected by the shared semi-sextile pinned by Sun and Venus. Of note here is that the learning triangle is retrograde, indicating that she will need to have more than one go at learning processes before they fall satisfactorily into place, that any searching and questing she does will be fuelled by the drive to learn, and that both of these figures link through her Sun to the Efficiency/Performance triangle and the tip of the arrow flying out to meet the "You".

"The Efficiency triangle has been the dominant aspect pattern for most of my life. It's the only figure in my natal chart that goes through the centre and is therefore capable of conditioning my whole character. Ego planets Sun and Moon are in it and Saturn connects to Moon/Mars at the apex. These are the first planets encountered by the environment. In many ways this triangle can be quite dysfunctional. The all-red aspects have a cardinal motivation but two of the planets involved are 'soft' planets – Moon and Neptune. Their motivation is for contact rather than action. Although the Sun is involved it's not very well placed for external action down in the 3rd house, so the energy build up in the opposition to feed the planets on the apex isn't all that it might be. That leaves Mars, which loves being in an achievement figure. However Mars is very closely conjunct the Moon, and for a long time that combination was frustrating for my Mars and scary for my Moon. There is a mix of energies in the Efficiency triangle so it is important that Saturn, which links to it, is a fixed planet, in a fixed sign and is well positioned in a fixed house."

When the distribution of planets in the Dynamic Curve is considered, both Mercury and Pluto are placed on Balance Points. Pluto can work efficiently, but is hampered by being intercepted so has to rely on Sun and the Venus/Jupiter conjunction to channel its energies. This could prove a source of frustration, especially if she feels her expressions of power can go unheard. The task here would be to use Pluto as an inner resource, allowing it to work cooperatively with her Sun but in a quieter and less obtrusive manner, in order to transform and refine her sense of self. Mercury is weak by sign, but with its linear red square to intercepted Uranus and its Balance Point position in the very small 4th house it is going to be kept busy and active.

> "If I had to pick a favourite planet in my chart it would be Mercury. It operates quite happily and although it's weak by sign I feel that's more than compensated for by the input from my intercepted Uranus which only has Mercury as an outlet. As Uranus is in the 8th house I think it feeds Mercury lots of inspiration and knowledge about what lies beneath the obvious and makes me quite skilled at reading between the lines. I think because Uranus is intercepted, Mercury sometimes gets overloaded and it can take a while to unscramble things that are coming through. Sometimes my Mercury just runs out of steam and dries up completely."

A theme emerges

At this point I want to highlight a recurrent theme I have found in Clara's charts. "Communication" kept coming up again and again, in different ways, as I went through them. Here are some of the pointers which have either already been mentioned, or are still to be considered:

- The implications of the separate linear square aspect between intercepted Uranus and Balance Point Mercury
- Jupiter/Venus are stressed before the 3rd house cusp; communication issues could be powered by intercepted Pluto so she could come on strong in this area of life. This could be added to by the placement of Jupiter/Venus in Aries, not a sign known for its reticence.

- Her Sun is in the 3rd house. It is strong by sign, just past the Low Point, so more optimistically placed, but considerable effort might be needed to strengthen and assume the full role of this planet.
- Sun is opposite Neptune, setting up conflict on the 3/9 Thought axis and possible confusion about her sense of self.
- The intersection of the Age Point in the natal and node charts also takes place on the 3/9 axis, indicating that related issues will be an on-going life theme.
- The Sun stays in the 3rd house in both the node and natal chart, making this an important area of life experience and expression and her Sun/sense of self a point of growth.

The Family Model in Clara's chart shows Sun as father in the 3rd house, an area of life associated with communicating to a wide range of people about a variety of subjects, and with the knack of having "the common touch." Sun is connected to Moon with a square aspect, indicating that a potentially gritty but inherently rewarding relationship could exist; both planets are part of the Efficiency triangle, and both aspect Neptune, so for Clara there could be feelings of ambivalence and confusion around her relationship with her father.

"As a vicar he was very much part of the 3rd house local community and living in a vicarage meant that our house was open to the whole community – there was rarely just our family there. Equally his position in the community had a Neptunian quality – he was their link to God after all! Whilst I have always admired my father immensely I felt as a child he had very little time for me emotionally (square to Moon) but over time that relationship has changed and our relationship now is very good – if not very emotional."

Saturn is strongly placed in a fixed sign in the fixed 2nd house, suggesting her mother provided a firm base, possibly within the home environment. I am curious to know if, during her upbringing, considerable attention was paid to security, to feeling safe and to not stepping outside the known limits and boundaries. Maybe her mother had to be austere and careful in managing the household budget, and had to keep things on a tight rein. Saturn and Moon are in opposition, indicating that the mother/child relationship could have been fraught with friction as Clara grew up. Yet with Moon and Saturn thus tied in a direct aspect, I would expect a lasting mother/child bond to remain; it will be interesting to discover how Clara experienced this as a child, and now as an adult. With her Moon the highest of the three ego planets, in conjunction with Mars in Leo, and placed at a distance from both Sun and Saturn, it could be that Clara felt something of a misfit within her family, as well as feeling there were high expectations placed upon her.

"Yes, things were tight financially when I was young and my mum taught me a lot about budgeting and also about prioritising, going without when you have to. For much of my life I found my Saturn quite an oppressive energy and there are links here with my relationship with my mother. My perception that 'life is hard', that the world is a potentially dangerous place and that when push comes to shove, you can only rely on yourself are all very similar to her view of the world, and indeed her mother's view of the world that she inherited. Having said that I've never been in any doubt about how much my mother loved me and she has always looked after me well in a physical sense – she still does!

I did feel something of a 'misfit' in our family and still do sometimes, learning to go my own way, developing my own values and ways of feeling secure has been something of a quest for me. However I've also learned that I can be 'different' and still be accepted and loved – which is very affirming."

Nodal · IC · Radix

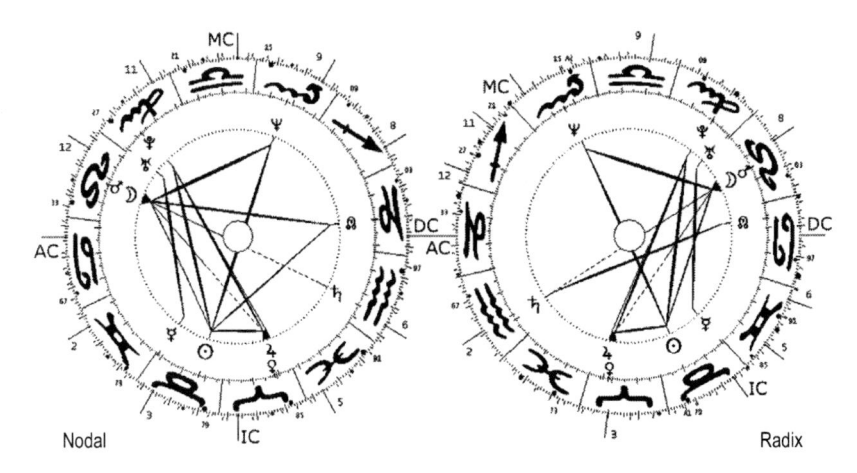

Clara's Moon Node and Natal Charts

Clara's moon node chart suggests that she comes from a more "I" sided approach to life, which may reinforce her feelings about the world being a potentially dangerous place where she needs to have her crossbow and arrow at the ready. The "You" side of her node chart is relatively empty, and we have to bear in mind that she may find it easier to relate to and express what this chart shows, falling back into familiar and well-worn ways of behaving.

Her Moon/Mars conjunction, hidden away in the 12th house in the node chart, rises to a much more prominent position in the 7th house of her natal chart. Her task is to no longer keep her feelings hidden, but to express them to the "You" out there in the world. Saturn has fallen from its nodal 6th house position and sits in the 2nd house of her natal chart. Here, her task is to draw on her understanding and her authoritative knowledge of service to others and put it to use in such a way that her own security can be taken care of at the same time. Immediately, her work in public service and local government, working in the service of others, comes to mind. Most interesting is her Sun; it and has not moved from its placement in the node chart, staying in the 3rd house in the natal chart. Once again there is a 3rd house focus, suggesting she has further work to do in this area of life experience and expression, with more to learn and more work to do on her Sun. The theme of communication is again highlighted, and as her Sun in both charts is opposite Neptune, confusion and a lack of clarity about her sense of self and how this is transmitted to the world could be significant issues.

"This very much links with past lives work I've done, where I had experience of energy flowing to the I-side, particularly the 12th house. My Sun staying in the 3rd house indicates that I have work to do on making a significant step in developing my own sense of identity and will. My Sun is very strong by sign but close to the low point of the 3rd house at the bottom of the natal chart, and I've come to realise that the development needs to be internal, for me, before being something I can express out in the world."

The crossing of the Age Points in Clara's natal and node chart also takes place on the 3/9 Thought axis. This shows a recurrent life theme of issues surrounding communication of all kinds. This theme could crop up again and again, each instance bringing with it the opportunity to learn more and refine her own ability to communicate. The meeting of these two Age Points took place in 1978, as the Age Point in both charts travelled through the 3rd house. Clara was then between 15 and 16 years of age, but the effects of this crossing point can be experienced over a period of up to two years either side of the exact point of the crossing. The first crossing point coincides with the movement of the Age Point coming into conjunction with her Sun. There is no way that such a coming together of energies, and the opportunity to learn about herself from them, could be ignored in someone as apparently self-aware as Clara is now. She has yet to reach the second crossing point, which will occur when her Age Point is in the 9th house, and if she has taken heed and learned from the lessons of the first crossing point in her mid-teens, the second crossing could be experienced as confirmation of being on the right track as well as bringing her an enlightened understanding of her life path.

Radix | House

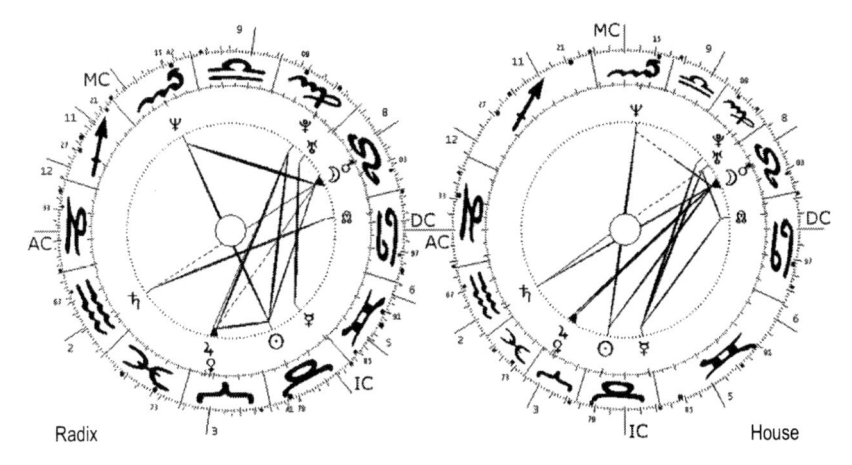

Clara's Natal and House Charts

The aspect structure in Clara's house chart appears "thinner" when viewed alongside her natal chart. It loses aspect patterns which are present in the natal chart but some new ones are introduced. Gone are the Search and Efficiency/Performance figures; the arrow has disappeared. In their place, the house chart shows an Ambivalence figure and a Small Learning triangle. Her fiery Moon/Mars at the tip of the arrow become the planets at the "escape" corner of the Ambivalence figure, where the two blue aspects meet. Was she expected and conditioned **not** to be active and not to make a fuss?

> *"What the world wants me to present are blue aspects and a blue Moon/Mars conjunction. I had lots of messages in my childhood about putting a good face on things, not letting people see when they'd upset me. One of my Mum's most used expressions was 'you can always think what you like', the clear implication being that it is generally best not to express it!"*

In the house chart, Clara's gain of the Small Learning triangle – direct, so the learning can take root quickly – incorporates the north node along with Uranus and Mercury. Perhaps this encourages her to learn how to communicate more successfully with the "You", without raising hackles or putting up backs?

"This seems to me to keep the benefits of the separate Uranus/ Mercury square but make it more flexible and responsive. I like the fact that in my house chart Pluto links in to that triangle via Mercury as I feel Mercury and Uranus cope better with the Pluto energy than my low point Sun, and particularly my stressed Venus."

The colour balance in her house chart offers additional blue which she may be able to draw upon when she needs to take things more easily, or give that red arrow a rest. But Clara will have to use this extra "blueness" with awareness. She will not be able to tap into it automatically as it is part of her conditioning and not inherent in her makeup. The additional blue could be a valuable resource, but it is only she who can choose to see it this way, act on it and use it with awareness in her life now.

Consideration of the Dynamic Calculations will add depth and further understanding of how Clara might have experienced her upbringing. As before, nothing should be regarded as set in stone, as the experience of the individual has to be taken into account and discussed with that person, as we are doing with Clara in this exploration of her charts.

	Total	Crosses - Motivation			Elements - Temperament			
		Car	Fix	Mut	Fire	Earth	Air	Water
Signs	104	23	67	14	45	32	14	13
House	139	41	61	37	6	32	58	43
Diff.	35	18	-6	23	-39	0	44	30

Clara's Dynamic Calculations

Clara's Dynamic Calculations give an overall stress score of +35. This is relatively high and is above the "comfort zone" score of +25, so within a range where she could feel uncomfortably pressured at times. Her own experience of what a score of +35 feels like is more valid than any assumptions I might make, although knowing the overall stress score gives me a clearer picture of how she might feel when pushed, and how she might use her crossbow and arrow as a defence mechanism to cope with the stress.

"My dynamic calculation score at +35 is quite high. I have a tendency to feel the world demands a great deal from me and that I'm never 'up to the job' always 'running to catch up', never quite able to provide what is required of me, never quite good enough. When I'm in situations that make me feel this way I usually 'run away' (back to the safety of a 12th house Moon in my nodal chart?). However, when cornered in these situations I do resort to using my 'bow and arrow' – I have a spectacularly violent temper as a last resort and, I'm told, very scary 'flashing eyes' when I'm close to letting rip – taking aim so to speak!"

The highest plus scores are found under Mutable (+23) and Air (+44), suggesting that she is expected to be more flexible than she can naturally be – probably quite a challenging task in itself for a fixed Taurean Sun. The +44 score in Air indicates that the environment may expect her to have a greater ability to communicate, express and articulate ideas than she has the inner resources to draw upon. Once again the theme of communication is woven into the fabric of Clara's chart and her life. With such a high plus score in Air, she could feel uncomfortable when she has to deliver or perform wherever communication is called for, and once again her crossbow and arrow could be used in self-defence.

Clara has more Fixity (-6) and a lot more Fire (-39) than the environment recognises or is interested in. With a high fixed minus score she is likely to need to know where she stands, to feel safe and secure and to preserve and maintain, reflecting the traits of her Taurean Sun and Saturn, a fixed planet in a fixed sign and house. She may be the one who insists on double checking and making sure all bases are covered; the environment may be less concerned with this, and will impatiently stand by as she goes through these checks. If hurried along, or ignored, she will feel misunderstood or frustrated, and maybe insecure. For someone with such a high minus score in Fire, it could be very hard for her to accept that people will not necessarily be as interested and enthusiastic as she can be. She might come across as intense or overwhelming when she gets the fiery bit between her teeth but the end result for her could be disappointment and feeling discouraged as the world will not want to receive the considerable quantity of fire energy that she wants to give.

> *"I have good communication skills – when I get to do it my way! I've always found it more difficult to communicate in styles imposed on me, academically for instance, or when I'm required to be entirely rational and logical. For me communication without passion (and perhaps direct feedback from others?) can be a stilted, unsatisfying business. I know others can find me overwhelming – at work I get teased about talking too much and 'going off on one' but equally I know that people value my enthusiasm. And yes, I get very frustrated if people don't care about things I think are important."*

At this point it is worth taking a look at the role the north node might play in Clara's life. It could provide the impetus to move her forward, and as she has indicated an interest and awareness of following a spiritual path of development, it would be appropriate to take this into consideration whilst looking at the benefits of connecting with her nodal axis.

Clara's north and south nodes span the 1/7 Encounter axis. This reinforces the opposition on this axis between Moon and Saturn which automatically sets up tension in the I/You area of her life. With her south node in the 1st house, Clara may be reluctant to commit fully to a one-to-one relationship, especially to one partner. There will be feelings of not wanting to throw her lot in with one other person and she may prefer to retain her own separate sense of self and her independence. With a 1st house south node there is an air of safety and a self-reliance to be gained from staying at arms length from a binding commitment, so how is this balanced out alongside her relationship with her partner and family? How difficult is it for her to accept this commitment, and if she does, how does the journey she has been through relate to her personal and spiritual growth? What has she learned about herself through her experiences in these areas of her life? A 7th house north node is going to demand a laying aside of her own personal, and some might say selfish, needs and tendencies in favour of putting herself last rather than first. The needs of others with whom she has close one-to-one relationships and connections will be treated with a higher priority. Although Clara might find this difficult, and at times even find herself resenting this, ultimately she will find a fulfilment in the inclusion of others which will enhance her interactions and enrich her 1st house sense of who she is.

The Moon/Mars tipped arrow points strongly to the 7th house, and there is no way that this area of life can be neglected or ignored. What she has to learn most about will be constantly laid before her in all manner of guises, and opportunities will present themselves for her to learn out there, in the field of human interaction, what developing her 7th house north node means for her.

> *"Commitment hasn't been something that's come easily to me but I have worked hard at this, at overcoming the fear it engenders in me, and I've been hugely rewarded for that effort with my children, partner and close friends. It's also one of the areas where I feel most proud of my achievements. I'm very clear now that I grow best (in terms of the vertical direction in my chart) when I do this with and through other people. If I want to come close to those Neptunian ideals of divine love and harmony I need to really know, and connect to, other people just as much as I need to know and connect with myself."*

Clara's Age Point is, at the time of writing, in the 8th house, in Virgo. Positioned between the Balance and Low Points, it is travelling through the fixed zone of the house, but is also conjunct Pluto. At the very time when her Age Point is in a fixed house zone and she might prefer not to be making significant changes in her outer life, the demands coming from inside could be very different. Pluto is a cardinal planet; it seeks to do, not to rest, and it embodies transformation, change and the shedding of old, outworn habits. It is intercepted in the sign of Virgo but significantly aspects Clara's Sun, drawing her inner attention firmly towards her self and how this might be changed, developed and transformed. It would be surprising if there were not strong inclinations around for her to make fundamental life changes.

Correspondingly, the Age Point in her node chart is making an active square aspect to Pluto, and a learning, searching quincunx to her Sun. We can regard the energies of the node chart as being less conscious, yet still significant as they are active beneath the surface and have a tendency to break through into consciousness bringing reminders of what is important right now. This is reflected back to us via the surrounding environment, sometimes in obvious but not always welcome ways. In Clara's case, there could be successive instances and experiences reinforcing the message of now being a time when transformation, change and possibly a deeper attunement to the spiritual path are called for.

> "I am very aware of the influence of Pluto in my life at the moment – it's intense, painful and terrifying but at some level I also know it's exciting. From my current position (which feels like a very small lifeboat in a very big and stormy sea!) there's not much more I can add yet – it's something that's in process."

Of additional significance there is Clara's age. She is nearly 45. Her Age Point is in the 8th house and is approaching the Low Point of the whole chart. This is a time when a re-evaluation of life is undertaken, so I would expect her to be taking stock of where she goes from here with her life, and that includes her family, her closest relationships and her career. I would expect some inkling of change in the offing to have been felt, and perhaps acted upon when, at age 43, her AP was conjunct Uranus. But that is likely to have been of less impact than her current life situation, where she could be more deeply engaged with an inner process of change and in making stronger connections to her own spiritual journey. I am interested to know how 8th house issues fit in here, too, as significant planets in the 8th house can be associated with making an important contribution to society.

> *"With my age point on Uranus I made some really hard decisions about re-prioritising in my life, refused promotion, down-sized to a 4 day week so I could do more astrology and other things I find fulfilling without eating into family/relationship time. This focussed on making the best use of my time and concentrating on what really matters. As it also coincided with me starting to teach astrology I think it was about making a different type of contribution linked to the more esoteric matters in the 8th house rather than the just through the more obvious 'social institutions' where I work."*

As I already know Clara is drawn to the spiritual path, it would be appropriate to discuss the seed thought for her ascendant sign with her. Her AC in earthy Capricorn reflects not only the earthiness of her Taurean Sun, which has been a significant factor throughout this appraisal of her chart, but also her current Age Point in Virgo, the other earth sign in the Zodiac. Earth confers sensuality and practicality; it works with what is, with matter and form, and it is reliable, solid and tangible. With this in mind, together with an appreciation of what is currently going on in her chart, it would be worth introducing to Clara the seed thought for Capricorn, *"Lost am I in light supernal, yet on that light I turn my back,"* to see if this has meaning for her, if it relates to her life at the present time, and if it hits a deep inner chord for her.

> *"For many years I had no sense of there being a 'light supernal', sometimes there wasn't even a light at the end of the tunnel! So I really struggled with this seed thought. As I've developed more trust and faith in the world around me that light has started to be revealed and I can see the temptation of getting 'lost' in it. However, I can also sense that this would be a form of escapism for me and maybe, given the 12th house emphasis in my nodal chart, something I've explored before. I feel very strongly that for me in this incarnation it is about interacting with the world and getting to grips with what it is to be human. So now I try to bathe in the 'light supernal' when I need to and let it support me as I go back and grapple with the challenges being human brings – as well as enjoying the pleasures!"*

Concluding Remarks

The two charts used here as examples are quite different, as are the people they belong to. By using and applying the techniques discussed in this workbook, it is possible to see how following the guidelines laid out in the Huber Method, and working with all three charts together, can yield a deep understanding of an individual's life journey.

So now it is over to you, the reader, student, seeker, astrologer. Using any astrological method and approach successfully, and with insight and responsibility, requires practise, experience and humility. As I said in the introduction to this book, the very best way to learn astrology and gain a deeper understanding of astrological psychology is to bring it to life and make it real. It has to live. It is all too easy to say that we know something about astrology and approach it from a mercurial, fact-finding place without it having that much bearing on reality. The Huber Method and the Jupiterian approach it takes offers endless opportunities to broaden our astrological understanding, making what we see, experience and understand in the charts we look at and work with both tangible and real. The birth chart can then become a living birth chart, full of potential for ongoing expansion, personal growth and spiritual development.

The astrologer Dane Rudhyar said *"No astrologer – and as well, no psychoanalyst – can interpret a life and destiny at a level higher than that at which he himself functions."* That alone serves as a reminder to aim high as we follow the ascending spiral of our own learning and searching, perfecting our understanding of ourselves along the way. What better way to do this than by using the Huber Method and working with our whole being using the three charts.

Bibliography

General Introduction to Astrological Psychology

The Cosmic Egg Timer, Joyce Hopewell & Richard Llewellyn
> Provides a general introduction to astrological psychology. Some familiarity with its subject matter will greatly enhance the reader's ability to gain benefit from reading *The Living Birth Chart*. There is valuable content related to each chapter. More detailed works related to specific topics in the various chapters are listed below.

Chapter 2 Seeing the Whole Person

Aspect Pattern Astrology, Bruno & Louise Huber, Michael Huber
> **The** reference work on aspect patterns.

Chapter 3 Integrating the Personality

Astrological Psychosynthesis, Bruno Huber
> Contains a major section on personality/ego integration.

The Planets and their Psychological Meaning, Bruno & Louise Huber
> Contains extensive material on the ego planets, plus a section on personality integration.

Chapter 4 Integrating with the Environment

The Planets and their Psychological Meaning, Bruno & Louise Huber
> **The** reference work on the Hubers' understanding of the psychological meaning of the planets. Includes a section on the Family Model.

Astrological Psychosynthesis, Bruno Huber
> Includes a section on the Family Model.

The Astrological Houses, Bruno & Louise Huber
> **The** reference work on the house system used by the Hubers, including the Dynamic Energy Curve, Balance Point, Low Point etc.

Transformation: Astrology as a Spiritual Path, Bruno & Louise Huber
> Good reference on the Dynamic House System, Dynamic Calculations, the House Chart and Stress Planets.

Chapter 5 Reconciling Past, Present and Future

LifeClock, Bruno & Louise Huber
> The reference work on the Hubers' approach to timing in the horoscope.

Moon Node Astrology, Bruno & Louise Huber
> The reference work on the Hubers' understanding of the Moon's nodes, the Moon Node Chart and its age progression, and working with three charts.

The Astrological Houses, Bruno & Louise Huber
> Includes definition of the polar axes in the chart.

Chapter 6 Following the Spiritual Path

Transformation: Astrology as a Spiritual Path, Bruno & Louise Huber
> Gathers together a number of the techniques pioneered by the Hubers related to personal and spiritual growth.

The Planets and their Psychological Meaning, Bruno & Louise Huber
> This reference work includes levels of the planets and the transpersonal planets.

Moon Node Astrology, Bruno & Louise Huber
> The reference work on the Hubers' understanding of the Moon's nodes and nodal axis.

Reflections and Meditations on the Signs of the Zodiac, Louise Huber
> Covers the Zodiac signs, their seed thoughts, and meditations using them.

Chapter 7 Working with the Three Charts

Moon Node Astrology, Bruno & Louise Huber
> Contains a chapter on consultation work using the three charts.

Contacts and Resources

The Astrological Psychology Institute (UK)

A MODERN APPROACH to SELF-AWARENESS and PERSONAL GROWTH

Astrology has become recognised as a valuable tool for the development of self awareness and human potential. Bruno and Louise Huber researched and developed this approach over many years, combining selective astrology with Roberto Assagioli's psychosynthesis. Our courses are based on their results and inspiration.

PERSONAL GROWTH Most of our Diploma students not only learn astrology, chart interpretation and astrological counselling skills, but find that the course helps develop their own self understanding and personal and spiritual growth.

COURSES We offer Foundation Modules to those new to astrology or to the Huber Method. Our Modular Diploma Course teaches the Hubers' psychological approach to chart interpretation for working with clients. Details are in our prospectus.

EVENTS Our programme of seminars, workshops and conferences includes annual workshops that are an integral part of the Diploma in Astrological Counselling.

CONJUNCTION Our magazine *Conjunction* contains articles, news and supplementary teaching materials.

API (UK) Enquiries and Membership
P.O. Box 29, Upton, Wirral CH49 3BG, England
Tel: 00 44 (0)151 605 0039; Email: api.enquiries@btopenworld.com
Website: www.api-uk.org

API(UK) Bookshop
Books and API(UK) publications related to the Huber Method.
Linda Tinsley, API(UK) Bookshop
70 Kensington Road, Southport PR9 0RY, UK
Tel: 00 44 (0)1704 544652, Email: lucindatinsley@tiscali.co.uk

---

API Chart Data Service
Provides colour-printed Huber-style charts and chart data.
Richard Llewellyn, API Chart Data Service
PO Box 29, Upton, Wirral CH49 3BG, UK
Tel: 00 44 (0)151 606 8551, Email: r.llewellyn@btinternet.com

---

Software for Huber-style Charts
AstroCora, MegaStar, Regulus, Regulus Light Special Huber Edition.
On CD: Elly Gibbs Tel: 00 44 (0)151-605-0039
            Email: software.api@btinternet.com
Download: Cathar Software Website: www.catharsoftware.com

Publications on Astrological Psychology

THE COSMIC EGG TIMER
A practical introduction to Astrological Psychology
by Joyce Hopewell & Richard Llewellyn

Introduces the Hubers' new and exciting way of using astrology, for all interested in finding out more about astrological psychology and themselves. Use your own birth chart alongside this book and gain insights into the kind of person you are, what makes you tick, and which areas of life offer you the greatest potential.

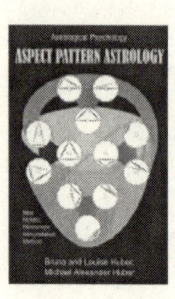

ASPECT PATTERN ASTROLOGY
Understanding motivation through aspect patterns

Essential reference work on this key feature of the Huber approach. The aspect pattern reveals the structure and basic motivations of our consciousness. Over 45 distinct aspect figures are identified, each with its own meaning. Whether beginner or experienced astrologer, aspect patterns can provide immediate significant revelations about yourself and others.

The Planets
and their Psychological Meaning

Shows how the positions of the planets are fundamental to horoscope interpretation. They represent basic archetypal qualities present in everyone, giving clues to psychological abilities and characteristics, growth and spiritual development. Comprehensive descriptions of each planet, based around fundamental principles aiming to stimulate interpretative abilities.

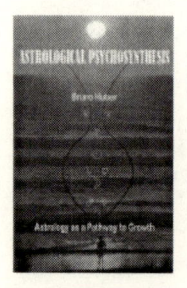

ASTROLOGICAL PSYCHOSYNTHESIS
Astrology as a Pathway to Growth

Bruno Huber's introduction to this holistic approach to astrology and Assagioli's psychosynthesis, following the premise that the soul is at the root of all developmental processes. The horoscope is used not just as an analytical tool, but also as an instrument to enhance the process of self-realisation and spiritual transformation. Three parts focus on intelligence, integration, relationships.

Books by Bruno & Louise Huber except where authors otherwise indicated.

A Modern Approach to Self Awareness and Personal Growth

MOON NODE ASTROLOGY

Combines psychological understanding with the concept of reincarnation, bringing a new astrological focus on the shadow personality and the individual's evolutionary process. Includes the psychological approach used with the Moon's Nodes and the Node Chart. Covers the role of three charts in the individual's evolutionary process, the Node Chart symbolising the past, the Natal Chart the present, and the House Chart the impetus from the environment for development.

LifeClock

The horoscope is seen as a clock for the person's lifetime, with the Age Point indicating their age as the 'time' on the clock. Those trying it invariably find significant correspondences between indications in their birth chart and meaningful events in their lives. This deepens self understanding and provides impetus and insight to psychological and spiritual growth. A powerful tool for the helping professions, enabling quick identification of psychological sources of a client's problems.

TRANSFORMATION
Astrology as a Spiritual Path

The last of the Huber books on astrological psychology to be fully translated into English. Describes processes of transformation and personal/spiritual growth as natural stages in human development, related to astrological indicators in the birth chart. Includes new material on Dynamic House System, Stress Planets, House Chart, and Integration Chart.

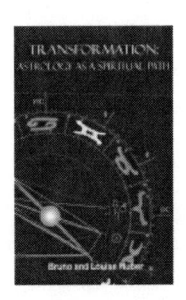

AstroLog I: Life and Meaning

There is now a substantial body of experience and knowledge in the use and refinement of the 'Huber Method' documented in the bi-monthly German-language magazine *AstroLog*. **AstroLog I** presents a selection of articles from this magazine, translated into English for the first time, on astrological psychology and its relevance to life and its meaning.

Published by HopeWell, PO Box 118, Knutsford, Cheshire WA16 8TG, UK

Printed in the United Kingdom
by Lightning Source UK Ltd.
134389UKBA/313-351/P